Zen Coffee

Books by Gloria Chadwick

Pen Stroke ~ A Novel Journey

*How to Write Your Book and
Get it Published The Write Way*

Novel Notes: 30 Days ~ 30 Chapters

*Magical Mind, Magical Life: How to Live a
Magical Life, Filled with Happiness and Light*

Zen Coffee: A Guide to Mindful Meditation

*Spirit to Self: Little Reminders of Who You
Really Are... A Powerful, Spiritual Being of Light*

Inner Journeys: Meditations and Visualizations

*Discovering Your Past Lives: The Ultimate
Guide Into and Through Your Past Life Memories*

Whispers Beyond the Rainbow: A Spiritual Quest

Somewhere Over the Rainbow: A Soul's Journey Home

Looking Into Your Future Lives: A Trip Through Time

The Complete Do-it-Yourself Guide to Past Life Regression

Zen Coffee

A Guide to Mindful Meditation

Gloria Chadwick

Mystical Mindscapes

Books to Enlighten and Empower

Zen Coffee

Publisher's Cataloging-in-Publication Data

Chadwick, Gloria

Zen Coffee: A Guide to Mindful Meditation

1. Meditation   2. Mindfulness
3. Zen   4. Coffee   I. Title

Library of Congress Catalog
Card Number: 2008932032

ISBN 10: 1-883717-62-0
ISBN 13: 978-1-883717-62-9

Mystical Mindscapes
Books to Enlighten and Empower

http://mysticalmindscapes.blogspot.com

This book is dedicated to Jaime

Contents

Zen Coffee uses coffee as a metaphor for meditating and tuning into the peaceful, calm essence of your inner nature as you zip through the Zen of daily life. It offers you ways to find a few moments every now and then to relax, to just breathe, and to get in touch with who you are.

There are meditations you can engage in with your eyes open and a cup of coffee in your hand. It plays off caffeine and how it both jazzes and calms your mind; this is similar to a Zen koan, which appears to be a paradox.

What mindfully meditating is all about and how to go about it. Filling your mind with meditation. Be here now. Breathe and be. Filling the essence of your inner self with coffee. Be with your coffee. Breathe in the aroma of your calm inner essence. Breathe and be.

A brief history of coffee, beginning with the goat shepherd, Kaldi, who discovered coffee and shared it with his friend, the

Capuchin monk whose robes were the color of a cup of cappuc-cino. This meditating monk shared coffee with his fellow monks to keep them awake during prayers.

Coffee was taken out of the realm of mindful meditation and made its way into Arabia and then later to Java. This book comes full circle, bringing coffee back into the realm of mindfully meditating.

The way you approach making coffee is the same way you can approach meditating in a mindful manner. Brewing the calm essence of your inner nature into the perfect cup of Zen coffee in a mindful manner.

Breathing and being with your Zen coffee. Drinking in the essence of your inner nature. Zen coffee allows you to focus in on the quiet calm in your cup of Zen coffee.

Roasting and blending the flavors of your inner essence into your cup of coffee. Making the best cup of mindful coffee. Getting the full flavor from meditating. Processing coffee beans to extract their inner essence.

The nature of coffee. The nature of your inner self. Espresso is the essence of coffee; the essence of your inner nature. The crema of coffee is the essence of mindfulness. Making the perfect shot of espresso. Making the perfect moment of mindfulness.

Being in a Zen garden of balance and harmony. Zen mindfulness—or meditating by coffee—expresses itself in a gentle frame of mind, a Zen peacefulness and harmony that flows naturally in and through your mind.

Endless choices: Creating your own cup of coffee to suit your taste; making meditation fit your lifestyle. A splash of happiness and calm included in your meditation can add joy and harmony to your life.

Coffee Quiz: Match your flavor, taste, and personality with your choice of coffee to show you your inner essence.

Using caffeine to wake up the calm, peaceful qualities of your inner self first thing in the morning.

Zen eye-openers. Drinking in your essence and taking in a shot of espresso to power your day. Meditating for a moment or two with your coffee to start your day off right.

Zen to go. Putting peaceful, positive thoughts into your mind. Coffee in your car as you drive to work and maneuver through traffic.

Zen coffee throughout the day to pace your activities through the ups and downs of life.

Walking with Zen. Bringing the essence of mindfulness with you into all your experiences. Being completely in the present moment, wherever you are, whatever you're doing.

Getting into the right frame of mind to tune into your peaceful, calm inner essence may seem a bit elusive and next to impossible in your busy, hectic day. Not so. Getting centered within the caffeine buzz to capture the essence of your inner nature in all your experiences.

Meditating on your coffee: Letting your mind float into the ethereal essence of the steam rising from your hot coffee. Breathe in the Zen. Tuning in and turning on your coffee maker—your inner self that creates the caffeine buzz in your life.

Calmly sitting and quietly enjoying a Zen coffee. How to quiet the zillion thoughts that constantly run through your monkey mind. Being present in every mindful moment can be a bit challenging as you chase the calm of Zen coffee.

Breathing and bringing your attention into the calmness and quiet of the present moment, into the gentle, peaceful essence of your inner nature.

Focusing on the present moment. Focused awareness through inner imagery and visualization to capture both the calm and the caffeine within your coffee. The essence of mindfulness is right here, right now, completely in the present moment.

Fifteen. There's No Time Like the Present 101

The present moment is where you find the peaceful essence of yourself. Mindfulness is a choice and an attitude. The present moment is a gift you give to yourself.

Returning your awareness to the present through a mantra of mindful meditation. Capturing the calm essence of your inner self in all your day-to-day experiences.

Alone at last; peace and quiet. A breather, a Zen coffee break; just you and your coffee. Enjoying a state of mind where you experience the joy and harmony of your inner self, where you can drink in the essence of your inner nature.

Finding a few moments every now and then to meditate and become mindful of who you really are. Creating a Zen space, a sanctuary where you can reconnect with yourself on an inner level to experience and enjoy the serenity, harmony, and flavor of your inner essence.

How can caffeine and calm, poured into the same Zen coffee cup, help you mindfully meditate? Ponder the koan as you grow your inner nature and expand it into the world around you. The duality of your inner nature and your outer experiences—being grounded while simultaneously reaching to attain enlightenment, peace, harmony, and joy, and to incorporate that peaceful essence into every part of your life.

Life lessons—what coffee can teach you. Self servings. The nature of Zen coffee beans. How to make every experience in your life a Zen cup of coffee as you minimize stress and maximize happiness.

Finding Zen in quiet hidden places in your mind where you never thought to look for them.

Putting the power of Zen into your life. Zen zippers; zipping into mindfully meditating. Mini meditations for everyone who takes their coffee, and situations in their life, maybe a bit too seriously. Zooming into the zest for Zen.

Grinding your own beans; processing mindfully before expressing what's on your mind. Creating your own meditations to fit your experiences in a mindful manner.

Filled to the brim. Frothing at the mouth. Steaming. Offers methods and mindful meditations for becoming and staying calm under pressure. The light, airy nature of Zen and mindfulness.

Making peace; experiencing harmony. Stirring loving kindness into the coffee cup of all your experiences to create a perfect blend of calm coffee flavored with peacefulness and kindness.

Making your life mindful in every moment. Flavoring all your experiences with Zen coffee.

Meditating with the Zen coffee guru—a wise teacher who gently leads you into the mindful awareness of your inner essence.

Introduction

You may be wondering how Zen equates with coffee. It may not be clear to you and your mind may be puzzling over the connection. If you are, you're in a Zen-like state, pondering this paradox of how caffeine combined with Zen meditation wakes up your mind while calming it at the same time.

This mindful quandary you've found yourself in is similar to a Zen koan, which is an enigma and seems to be an oxymoron. A koan is a Zen Buddhist riddle that is used to focus the mind during meditation; it is something that has no easy answer and may be totally illogical in nature. It's something you can't easily wrap your mind around.

A koan is a question that must be experienced in order to be understood. A koan reveals itself in a moment of satori, a state of enlightenment or spiritual insight where an intuitive, instant understanding comes to you without words or thought processes. This is where Zen comes into your coffee.

You may still be thinking that Zen and coffee don't really mix. Or do they? Caffeine and calm, poured into the same coffee cup, seem to be totally contradictory to one another. That's the koan, the seemingly unsolvable mystery or riddle. Perhaps if you meditate on it a bit while sipping your coffee, the answer will come to you.

Zen and coffee are opposites that would appear to be never in balance or harmony. Zen is powerful and peaceful, gentle and strong at the same time. Coffee is strong and soothing, relaxing and invigorating at the same time.

Can you be Zen-like and meditate as you're zipping through your daily life on a caffeine high? Can you be fully here now in the present moment when your mind is scattered in several different places at once, going in various directions?

Can coffee help you gather your thoughts and clear your mind as you calm and center yourself? I say yes. Yes, because your mind is always connected to the essence of your inner nature. You can center your awareness within the peaceful essence of your inner nature as you embrace the Zen of coffee.

Zen meditation is pure and simple; it's accomplished by sitting quietly, clearing and stilling your conscious mind by not allowing your thoughts to wander or intrude while letting your mind empty itself.

If a conscious thought enters your awareness, you acknowledge it as merely a thought and gently let it go, without attaching any feelings to it, giving it any importance, or thinking about it.

You simply allow your mind to be quiet. The objective is to reach a state of nirvana [the attainment of enlightenment and the freeing of yourself from attachment to worldly things] nothingness where you transcend the physical and you're aware of everything, understanding it completely within your mind as you achieve a state of divine awareness of your inner nature.

A more active form of Zen meditation embraces mindfulness—your thoughts are completely in the present moment;

you're totally aware of where you are, what you're doing, how you're feeling, and you're accepting what you experience without judgment. This keeps you centered and connected with your current emotions and experiences.

Mindfulness is first accomplished by simply breathing and being aware that you're breathing. Your breath brings your awareness into the present moment, centering you completely into right here, right now.

The objective is to again reach a level of nirvana [the attainment of a completely enjoyable moment that provides the embracing of an ultimate experience of harmony or joy] which allows you to tune into the calm, peaceful essence of your inner nature.

You can incorporate both forms of mindful meditation into a Zen coffee. How often, while drinking a cup of coffee, have you spaced out, letting your thoughts go completely, emptying your mind and simply enjoying your coffee and a peaceful feeling of just being? You were mindfully meditating, filling your mind completely in the present moment, letting go of all other thoughts except what you were experiencing with your coffee.

Perhaps you focused on the warmth of the cup in your hand and tuned into the aroma and steam rising from the coffee. Perhaps the warmth of the coffee soothed your spirit. Perhaps you perceived the steam as an ethereal wisp of your inner nature, letting the aroma of the coffee and the peacefulness of your inner essence completely engulf you.

Or perhaps you drank it down without a second thought. Even quickly slurping a cup of coffee provides you with an opportunity to transcend your physical nature and the everyday world for a time, if you will take a mindful moment to be aware of and enjoy your coffee.

Drinking coffee in a Zen moment transports you into a meditative frame of mind where you are completely in the present moment. Just like the steam rising from your hot coffee, you can rise into the ethereal essence of your inner nature.

Quietly sipping your coffee offers you time for yourself, a nurturing respite from your busy lifestyle. The quiet time you spend for reflection and introspection brings relaxation and refreshment to your mind; it offers you a nice and much-needed breather to get into the calm, peaceful essence of you.

You can sit in solitude in a Zen-like state of meditation with your coffee to ease and erase the stresses and strains of your everyday experiences with the warmth, taste, and aroma of your coffee as you nurture the inner essence of you.

The quiet, meditative moments you spend in this manner bring you peace and serenity. It is here—in this quiet time and meditative place of peace and harmony within yourself, that you become in tune with your inner essence—with the true nature of you.

This works wonderfully well if you can find a few moments for yourself to sit in silence and just be with yourself. If you can't, you can still tune into yourself with a cup of coffee in any situation you find yourself in. This is how the Zen of coffee works. You can achieve many peaceful moments of harmony while you're on the go and racing around, running through life.

Coffee gives you a quiet time, a moment or two every now and then, scattered here and there, to de-stress and drink in the mindfulness of Zen; to relax and reflect; to go within your inner essence to replenish yourself and refresh your mind.

Zen Coffee is for people on the go; it offers an active approach to mindfully meditating in every moment of your busy life. It offers you many ways to bring peace and a sense of serenity into all your experiences and activities, to be in harmony with them. As you race through life with your coffee cup in hand, you'll find many mindful moments to meditate.

This book uses coffee as a metaphor for meditating and tuning into your inner nature as you zip through the Zen of daily life to tune into and embrace the peaceful essence of your inner self.

It offers you ways to find a few moments every now and then to relax, whether you're alone or with other people, whether you're feeling calm or are in a stressful situation. There are meditations interspersed throughout the book that you can engage in with your eyes open and a cup of coffee in your hand.

Zen Coffee shows you how to tune into and be in touch with your inner nature as it invites you to drink in the Zen of your spirit. Tuning into the essence of your calm, peaceful inner nature is as quick and easy as drinking your coffee and being mindful as you race through the ups and downs of your experiences.

A few moments of mindfulness scattered here and there puts the caffeine calm of Zen coffee into your life.

Chapter One

Mini Mindful Meditations

Breathing is something you do every day, day in and day out. So what makes breathing so special, other than keeping you alive? It's when you focus on your breath, when you're completely aware that you're breathing in and out.

This is mindfulness, paying attention only to your breath. It centers you within yourself, calms your mind, and opens you to your inner nature. It brings you into harmony and creates peacefulness.

Breathe. Be here, now, completely in the present moment. Let your thoughts go as you center into what you're doing and feeling at this very moment. Breathe and be.

Being in the present moment is stilling and empowering. It is mindfulness, being mindful of what you're doing in the moment that you're doing it, without letting your thoughts wander.

If your thoughts stray, gently focus your awareness on your breathing, into the present—right here, right now—into what you're doing and feeling at this exact moment in time. Just breathe and be with yourself.

In Zen meditation, a bell is used to bring your awareness back into yourself. When you hear the bell, you stop what you are doing and focus completely in the present moment. You use your breath to bring you into the peaceful essence of your inner self.

Let coffee be your bell to meditate. Whenever and wherever you are, whatever you are doing and feeling, as you drink your coffee, let it bring you fully into the present moment, into the awareness of your calm, peaceful inner nature.

Mindfulness meditation is simply being here now, in the present moment. Breathe and be. Just breathe and be. That's all you have to do.

Focus your complete attention and awareness on your breathing; think only of your breathing. Feel your breath coming into your body, then gently leaving your body. Breathe in. Breathe out. Breathe.

By simply breathing and being aware of your breath, you will reduce stress and be revitalized. At different times during your day, be mindfully present in the moment of here and now.

Breathe and focus your attention on your breathing. Let your breath bring you into the present moment, into the essence of your inner nature. Breathe.

That's what mindful meditation is. You can accomplish the same thing with a Zen coffee meditation, being completely mindful of your coffee.

Breathe. Breathe in the present moment; breathe in the aroma of your coffee. Let it fill your mind with its fragrant aroma. Breathe out your thoughts. Let your mind be still. Breathe in the essence of your coffee. Let your mind focus only on what you are experiencing with your coffee.

Breathe. Be here now in the present moment with your coffee. Be present with your coffee. Breathe in the aroma of your coffee, breathe out the essence of your coffee. Be in tune with your coffee; be in tune with the essence of your inner nature.

Breathe in the peaceful essence of your inner self; feel it flowing through your body and your mind.

Breathe out the aroma of your inner self, breathing and being completely in tune with yourself, breathing and being completely in the present moment.

Breathe and be with your coffee. Breathe and be with yourself.

Chapter Two

More Than You Wanted to Know About Coffee

A brief history—not always accurate—of coffee's journey from birth into your coffee cup begins with the Ethiopian goat shepherd, Kaldi, who discovered coffee by accident. One day the grazing goats he was calmly tending on the side of a mountain became quite rambunctious, frolicking with boundless energy.

At first Kaldi was concerned about his goats, thinking they were somehow possessed. He watched them closely the next morning and discovered that upon awakening, they were just like you and me first thing in the morning—a little cranky, feeling a bit disoriented, and not yet up to being fully awake.

The sleepy goats wandered around for a while, washing up in the nearby creek and taking care of bodily functions. A little later in the morning, all the goats, seeming to somehow communicate telepathically with one another, decided to take a coffee break, to gather at the coffee tree.

Kaldi noticed them sneaking behind some bushes and eating the berries from a nearby tree. After ingesting the berries, which we now know are coffee beans, the goats became enlivened before Kaldi's eyes, jumping for joy, happy to be awake and alive on such a beautiful day.

Little did the goats of Ethiopia know that they were starting a trend that is still with us today—the morning ritual of coffee. Kaldi, being a good goat shepherd who shared everything with his goats, was a bit miffed that they had not included him in their coffee break. So he walked over to the coffee tree and tried a few berries himself. Soon he was prancing about the mountain with his goats, dancing for joy at this wonderful treat that had been discovered.

A few days later, a gentle, calm, elderly Capuchin monk was meditating on the mountain, seeking enlightenment. He saw Kaldi and his goats dancing on the mountain, shouting with joy.

He thought perhaps this was a new form of meditation because it brought joy and harmony to Kaldi and his goats, which is the goal of meditation.

It appealed to him because the prayers at the monastery were quite boring, putting him and the other monks to sleep; none were attaining enlightenment this way.

He reverently approached the caffeinated shepherd as one would approach a spiritual guru and asked very politely and humbly to be shown the way to this most wondrous form of enlightenment.

Kaldi, being a generous soul, shared the secret with the monk whose robes were the color of a cup of cappuccino, going over to the coffee tree and pulling some of the berries off to give him. Thus began the second ritual of coffee—sharing a cup over conversation.

Actually, it wasn't exactly a cup of coffee—it was more like crunching the coffee beans with his new friend. After having coffee, this meditating monk felt much younger than his many years and had more energy than he could ever remember.

He was absolutely delighted with this new form of meditation. It allowed him to think clearly, so he called it mindful meditation. [Not true, but it sounds good in this story and fits in with the theme of this book.]

Wanting to share this wondrous way to enlightenment, he brought some berries from the coffee tree to his fellow monks to keep them awake during prayers.

Soon the word spread to other monasteries and many monks made the pilgrimage to the mountain to obtain the coffee berries. Monks believed that the coffee plants were holy, linked to the essence of spiritual matters.

A short time after the original discovery, as the elderly Capuchin monk was enjoying his coffee beans and mindfully meditating, he listened to an idea that had been brewing in his mind. It was a satori moment, a burst of enlightenment, no doubt brought on by the coffee.

His brilliant thought was that he and his monk brothers could create a beverage from the coffee berries, using fresh, hot, steamy, frothy milk from the goats. Hence the drink, cappuccino, came into existence. [Also not true.]

The timeline is a little off here. While Capuchin monks did create the first cappuccino, it happened in Italy, not Ethiopia, and it wasn't made with goat's milk. For all anyone knows, the cappuccino-creating monks were direct descendants of the first monk to taste coffee.

Perhaps the thought of a coffee drink was received in a mindful state of meditation in which the elderly monk communicated with his fellow Capuchin monks a century or so later.

Coffee was taken out of the realm of mindful meditation—and out of the hands of the Capuchin monks—by Ethiopian warriors who stumbled upon the coffee berries before they invaded Arabia (now called Yemen), bringing with them some of the mystical seeds.

The Arabs, not being alcohol drinkers, were enamored of the coffee berries that, in their opinion, were similar to the intoxicating effects of alcohol. Because Kaldi and the Capuchin monk didn't know what to call this spiritual coffee berry, the Arabs, in their native Arabic language, named it qahway (KAH wah), meaning "Arab's wine." They were the first to cultivate coffee plants, creating the coffee known as Arabica.

About the same time, a man named Ali bin Omar al-Shadhili was banished to Yemen because he fell in love with the king's daughter. After drifting aimlessly for a few days, he wandered into a Capuchin monastery. Perhaps the monks felt sorry for him, having lost the love of his life, and shared the berries with him.

Thinking that coffee was the way to his love's heart, he brought some coffee berries back to the kingdom, curing the people of sickness by giving them coffee. He was pardoned and named patron saint of coffee growers and drinkers, not to mention he got the girl of his dreams.

Enter the Arabian nomads into the picture. They used the coffee berries to make a solid, food-like substance, mixing them with meats, fats, and beans to form a hard, oval-shaped cake, similar to a high-energy trail mix bar, which they took with them on their journeys.

The caffeine in the coffee berries kept the nomads awake during their long travels, much in the same way that coffee keeps us awake when we are driving long distances.

The Arabs, both the warriors and the nomads, were highly superstitious about their coffee plants, believing that the berries had mystical powers. Under penalty of terrible things happening, such as the seeds not germinating, they showed the plants to no one, not sharing their secret with the rest of the world.

Then a man named Sygloud Badu Budam, after vacationing in Arabia and discovering the secret on an early-morning jaunt, smuggled seven seeds into India. The trees grew like wildfire, convincing the Indians that the plants were indeed magical and even a bit mysterious, both because of their taste and their re-generative powers.

After coffee came out of hiding in Arabia and blossomed in India, it made its way into the Dutch colony of Java, where again the coffee trees blossomed and were revered, taking on a new, distinctive taste known as Java.

The Dutch, being very creative people and wanting to mix things up, mixed the two coffees together to make Mocha Java, the first coffee blend.

By the way, at this point in time, Mocha wasn't synonymous with chocolate yet and hadn't taken on the familiar trappings of the coffee drink called Mocha. Mocha is a port city in Arabia where coffee was exported from. The Dutch, in addition to mixing things up, introduced the first coffee beans into Europe.

Coffee gravitated and grew into royalty in France. A coffee plant sent to Amsterdam spawned a seedling that was sent to Paris. When it arrived, it was given to King Louis XIV, who spent his days meditating and staring at the plant, sending it love-vibes, but wanting to keep coffee all to himself.

Somehow the coffee tree escaped from its prison in the Jar-din Des Plantes (garden of plants). It's rumored that Gabriel de Clieu, a seafaring captain, persuaded a high-ranking woman of the French court to steal a seedling from Louis XIV's plant. He shared the love; all American coffees are descended from the same tree that was closely guarded in Paris.

He sailed from France with the seedling, which he took up to the deck for its daily dose of sunlight. During the voyage there was a water shortage and Gabriel, an angel of sorts who loved his coffee plant, shared his small ration of water with it to keep it alive.

The Caribbean islands received a stolen sprout from the tree after it survived its long trip across the ocean into a new world. Brazil obtained coffee plants when an army officer named Francisco de Melo Palheta seduced the French governor's wife during an arbitration of a border dispute between Dutch Guiana (known today as Suriname) and French Guiana.

At the end of the meetings to resolve the dispute, the governor's wife presented Francisco with a bouquet of flowers in which five coffee seedlings and 30 fertile coffee seeds were concealed. Her husband never knew about it. The coffee, that is.

The Germans stole the coffee seeds from the Dutch. Shortly after its arrival, coffee was banned in Germany because it was thought to cause sterility. The musical composer, Johann Sebastian Bach, who definitely wasn't sterile, having fathered twenty children, wrote his "Coffee Contata" in protest.

The Germans then planted their pilfered seeds, after it was discovered how fertile coffee really is, in Kenya, 100 miles south of Ethiopia, where the coffee plants were originally discovered by Kaldi's goats.

Along the way, coffee made some interesting side trips. It was both revered and reproached. Sometime in the 1500s, coffee houses began opening their doors all over the world, becoming a gathering place to meet with friends.

Kair Bey, governor of Mecca, used his authority to ban the drinking of coffee and coffee houses, believing them to be places of rowdy disorder and hot spots of sin, inspiring such irreverent activities as singing and dancing.

He made the fatal mistake of telling the sultan of Cairo, a coffee lover who re-opened the coffee houses, causing his people to sing and dance with joy. It's said that Kair Bey lost his head shortly after.

In Turkey, as coffee houses opened in proliferation, preachers and government officials became very nervous and declared coffee sinful and unlawful. All coffee houses were closed and coffee was strictly forbidden.

Kuprili, Grand Vizier of Constantinople, ordered that anyone caught drinking coffee be tied into a sack and thrown into the sea. In Venice, coffee was persecuted by the Council of Ten, who banned coffee houses on the grounds that they were immoral, vice-ridden, and corrupt.

But that didn't stop dedicated coffee drinkers, among them an Italian priest, who was probably related to the first Capuchin monk whom Kaldi had shared his coffee with. Perhaps he was the one who made the first cappuccino.

Some of his not-so-enlightened fellow priests, after tasting the delicious brew, urged the Pope to ban coffee as Satan's substitute for wine. The Pope, being fair minded, tried the coffee and liked it so much that he blessed and baptized the coffee beans as a gift from God.

In England, Charles II denounced coffee houses as meeting places for dissidents and subversives who spread scandalous rumors that may or may not have been true about His Majesty and His Court.

Charles revoked the licenses of the coffee houses, ordering them to close in two weeks. Coffee lovers revolted, rising up against this outrageous opposition and Charles, under pressure, withdrew the order in eleven days.

From England, coffee traveled to America, where the first coffee house, named the Green Dragon, opened at 80-86 Union Street in Boston in 1697.

No matter what was said or done, coffee houses survived and today there is probably one right around the corner from you.

Which brings us to right here, right now, in the present moment, into Zen Coffee, bringing coffee full circle from Kaldi and his goats, and the elderly Capuchin monk, back into the realm of mindful meditation.

Chapter Three

Brewing the Perfect Cup of Zen

Brewing your coffee is the first step in mindful meditation as you brew the essence of your inner nature into the perfect cup of Zen coffee.

The way you approach making your coffee is the same way you approach meditating. You can brew the perfect cup of Zen coffee in a mindful manner.

Zen is simplicity personified with attention to subtle detail. It's the true nature of meditating in a mindful manner. Being mindful of how you make your coffee shows you how to be mindful in every part of your life.

Brew the best cup of coffee and experience the best kind of meditation by being mindful, by being completely here now in the present moment, focusing and centering your attention exclusively on what you are doing and feeling.

Drip brewing the perfect cup of coffee starts with the freshest whole beans. Zen coffee starts with being mindful of the freshness and inherent clarity of your mind to bring you into the essence of your inner self.

Use whole beans and grind them at home just before you make your coffee. Grind the beans to fit the type of coffee maker you have, being mindful of the nature of meditation.

The type of grind will determine the finished result. If the grind is too coarse, there is less surface area on the bean and the coffee will be weak because the water will pass through too quickly. If you rush meditation, you will pass through it too quickly and not achieve the full flavor of mindfulness.

If the grind is too fine, the coffee will be bitter and unpleasant. If you sift through every thought and feeling you have while you are mindfully meditating, your meditation experience will not be pleasing. By having the perfect grind, you will have the perfect flavor of a mindful meditation experience.

Use the best coffee filters. When you're meditating, filter out anything that causes a disturbance or distracts you. You can only get the best cup of Zen coffee, the best mindful meditation, by filtering out your conscious mind's noise and the outside distractions that interfere with your peaceful Zen moment.

Filtering keeps out what you don't want to intrude, just as a coffee filter keeps out the grounds from your cup of coffee. You don't want grounds in your coffee; this would be an unpleasant experience and would intrude on the enjoyment of your coffee.

While you are meditating, you don't want intrusions; you want your mind to be still, to listen to the silence so you can hear the quiet peacefulness of your inner nature and enjoy your meditation experience.

Use pure water to make your coffee. Use pure, clear thoughts while meditating. Coffee is actually 98.7 percent water. It's the coffee bean and the type of grind that makes a perfect cup of coffee.

Mindfulness is that special 1.3 percent essence that makes the perfect meditation. The water—a symbol of your subconscious—is the vehicle through which you experience the essence of the coffee itself, the essence of your inner self.

The temperature of the water is very important; how and when you choose to meditate is important because it determines whether your Zen meditation experience is a delicious cup of perfectly-brewed coffee, a lukewarm cup lacking flavor, or a too-hot cup which tastes burned.

Use hot water, not boiling. Coffee is best when brewed at temperatures between 195 and 200 degrees; this brings out the richest flavor in the coffee bean. Achieving mindfulness wherever you are, wherever you go, whatever you're doing, brings out the richness of your inner self.

Use a coffee maker with a slow brew time; the optimum is between four and seven minutes. Take your time when you meditate; give yourself a slow brew time to go within for the optimum experience. Measure your coffee by using two heaping tablespoons of ground coffee for every eight ounces of water.

Measure your mindfulness as your coffee brews, giving yourself the right measure of time to meditate. Too little time and the coffee is watery and diluted; too much time and the coffee is too strong.

Too little time to meditate and your meditation is lacking. Too much time and your thoughts will wander as you wonder why you're meditating. Balance your meditation time to brew the perfect cup of Zen coffee so you get the full flavor from meditating without overdoing it.

Be mindful as you brew your coffee. Breathe. Look at the shimmering coating on the coffee beans; feel their texture in your hand as you put them into the grinder. Breathe. Hear the noise the grinder makes as it grinds the beans. Breathe.

Smell the aroma from the freshly-ground coffee beans that envelops you as you put them into the coffee filter. Breathe in their deep, rich, intense fragrance.

Notice the color, the texture of the ground beans, the way they look in the coffee filter. As you pour the pure water into your coffee maker, notice the clearness of the water, hear the gurgling sound. Breathe.

As you plug in your coffee maker, notice the light that goes on. Breathe. Listen to the first drops of water as they sizzle into the carafe; notice the color of the coffee. Breathe. Watch the steam that rises, swirling in the carafe; be mindful of the ethereal nature of your inner self.

Smell the first delicious whiff of your coffee as it begins to brew. Listen to the sounds the coffee maker makes as it brews your coffee. Breathe.

Listen to the sounds of your inner self as you're waiting for your coffee to finish brewing. Breathe. Breathe and be with the essence of your coffee, with the essence of you.

When the coffee is done brewing, let it sit for a moment or two to attain its full flavor. Don't rush your meditation. Let yourself sit for a moment or two to obtain the full flavor of meditating.

Now you have a perfect cup of Zen coffee, a perfect mindful meditation you can enjoy and savor, just like your rich, aromatic cup of coffee.

Chapter Four

Drinking in the Essence of Zen

Coffee tastes best when it is fresh; when you drink it a moment or two after brewing. Meditation is best experienced when you freshly brew the moment, when you drink in the essence of your inner self after mindfully making your coffee.

Now that your coffee is perfectly brewed, you can fully enjoy and experience your coffee; you can fully enjoy and experience the essence of your peaceful inner nature that you've brought forth by simply breathing and being in the present moment with your coffee. Breathe.

Feel the handle of the carafe in your hand; notice its weight, the amount and color of the coffee inside. Breathe. Feel the motion of your arm as you pour the coffee into your cup. Breathe. Hear the liquid sound and smell the aroma as you fill your cup with coffee.

See the steam rising from your cup of coffee. Be aware of yourself putting the carafe back on the burner. Breathe in the wonderful aroma of your freshly-made coffee. Breathe in the essence of your coffee as you breathe in the essence of your inner self.

If you put cream and sugar in, notice the color and texture of the cream and sugar as they blend and dissolve into your coffee. Look at the change in the color of your coffee. Breathe.

Feel the spoon in your hand as you stir your coffee, as you blend the sweetness and lightness into your Zen coffee. Breathe. Be aware of the mindful process you've experienced in brewing and pouring your coffee.

Now comes the best part—drinking your coffee. Hold your steaming mug of coffee in both hands and deeply breathe in the aroma of your freshly-brewed cup of coffee. Feel the essence of the aroma in your mind. Deeply breathe in the ethereal essence of you.

Feel the cup in your hands, its texture and shape; feel its warmth from the coffee inside. As you raise your cup of coffee to your mouth, be aware of the motion of your arms. Breathe in the aroma and warmth of your coffee.

As you take that first delicious sip, notice the taste, the flavor of your coffee; notice how the coffee feels in your mouth. Notice the warmth, feel it moving into your throat as you swallow. Breathe. Feel the essence of the coffee within you. Experience the essence of your coffee, the essence of you. Breathe and be with your coffee. Breathe and be with yourself.

Take a moment to breathe in the Zen and to feel the calm, peaceful essence of Zen within you. Enjoy your hot cup of java while you mindfully meditate on the steam rising from your coffee, just like the ethereal essence of your inner self arising within you.

Feel your Zen nature within you. Breathe in the Zen. Breathe in the essence of your inner self. Breathe out the essence of your coffee. Breathe out the ethereal essence of your spirit, allowing it to permeate everything around you and within you.

While mindful meditation, when you're first beginning, is more easily achieved in a quiet place in your home, you can experience mindful meditation at a coffee house while you're waiting for your coffee drink to be made and served.

Even though there are many more distractions, you can be mindful in much the same manner as when you brew your coffee at home. In truth, the coffee house distractions are all part of being in the present moment, of mindfully meditating on your coffee house experience.

Breathe in the aroma of the coffee house as you walk through the door. Breathe deeply of the rich, flavorful coffee scent in the air that wafts through your mind, that stirs through your soul.

Notice what you think and feel as you're smelling the coffee. Breathe and be fully in the present moment. Completely experience this Zen coffee moment as you breathe in the essence of the aroma of the coffee house.

Breathe in the experience of the coffee house. Listen to and be fully aware of all the sounds in the coffee house, simultaneously and separately. Hear them with your mind and with the essence of your inner self. Breathe.

Hear the sound of the espresso machine as the coffee beans are ground fresh for each drink. Breathe. Listen to the gurgling, hissing, spitting sounds as the milk is steamed for coffee drinks. Breathe in the sounds around you.

Listen to the hum of conversation; hear it as soothing music, much like a gentle waterfall that soothes you into a Zen moment. Breathe. Breathe and be in this moment as you're waiting for your coffee drink to be made and served.

Be aware of yourself walking over to the coffee bar to pick up your drink. Feel the warmth of the cup in your hand as you raise it to your mouth.

As you take that first delicious sip, notice the taste, the flavor of your coffee; notice how the coffee feels in your mouth, notice the warmth, feel it moving into your throat as you swallow. Breathe.

Feel the essence of the coffee within you. Enjoy your coffee. Experience the essence of your coffee, the essence of you. Breathe and be in this Zen coffee moment.

The Zen of coffee allows you to mindfully meditate, anywhere, at any time, wherever you are, and whatever is happening all around you. Zen coffee allows you to focus in on the quiet calm of your coffee.

Simply Being Zen

Just being Zen.

Just breathing.

Just being.

Just Zen.

Simply. Being. Zen.

Take a quiet moment, with or
without coffee, to go within and enjoy
a peaceful moment all to yourself.

Simply be. Zen.

Chapter Five

Brewing the Coffee of Mindfulness

Brewing the perfect cup of coffee starts with the best coffee beans. Brewing the perfect meditation starts with the best of your inner nature that you give yourself. There are two types of coffee beans—Arabica and Robusta.

You have two choices in meditating—whether to be mindful or to not be present in the moment. When you are meditating, you have choices in the quality and flavor of your meditation, and in how you meditate.

Better coffee comes from the Arabica beans; they are much more flavorful than the Robusta beans. Arabica beans are grown at higher elevations than Robusta. Cooler weather at the higher elevations in the mountains cause the beans to take longer to mature, thus intensifying their flavor.

Perhaps this is why the Capuchin monks meditate at higher levels of elevation; it raises their thoughts and produces a more flavorful meditation.

Growing your Zen meditation practice occurs in the higher elevations of your mind as you grow into the awareness and essence of your peaceful inner nature.

Harvesting the coffee beans is a mindful process, taking care to select only the best, ripe beans. Harvesting your inner nature into your life is a mindful process of selecting the right way for you to meditate and blending the process of meditation into your lifestyle.

Just-picked green coffee cherries have to be processed to separate the core green bean from the red fruit that surrounds it. When you begin to meditate in a mindful manner, you have to process and separate your thoughts to get at their core, to reach their divine simplicity, to extract the inner essence of you.

Processing coffee beans extracts and brings forth their inner essence, just as meditating extracts and brings forth your inner essence. There are two types of processing: wet or washed, and dry processing, just as there are two ways to mindfully meditate.

You can meditate in a fluid manner, going with the flow of the moment, flowing with your feelings, or you can meditate in the warmth of the light of your mind, basking in your peaceful inner essence. Both work equally well with slight differences.

Wet processing involves cutting the skin of the coffee cherries, allowing the remaining fruit to ferment until the skin can be easily washed off. You can cut through the outer, extraneous portion of the mundane world and wash it away to clear your mind. This exposes the beans, which are then dried. In the process of meditation, you reach the core of your inner essence. This method retains the perfect clarity and sweet brightness of the natural flavors of the coffee.

Dry processing involves allowing the coffee cherries to dry naturally in the sun until they can be cracked open to reveal the bean inside. By allowing the light of your peaceful inner self to permeate your essence, you naturally open to your true nature. This method produces coffees that taste more earthy and com-plex. While meditating, you can be down to earth while achieving a more complex, inner state of mind at the same time; this is part of your dual nature—physical and spiritual—and is part of the koan of meditating by coffee.

After the coffee beans are picked and processed, they're roasted to enhance their natural essence and to develop their maximum flavor. After you've begun to meditate, you will intuitively fine-tune and enhance the way you meditate to bring the full flavor of mindfulness into all your experiences.

As you grow your Zen practice of mindfully meditating, you will fully develop and enhance your awareness of the essence of your peaceful inner nature. You'll roast and blend the flavors of your inner essence into the coffee cup of your life.

The first roasting of coffee beans was begun in 1662 in Europe with the beans being roasted and toasted over charcoal fires without flames, in ovens and on stoves, browned in uncovered earthenware tart dishes, old pudding pans, and fry pans. Roasting was trial and error, a hit or miss method, searching to find the perfect way.

Half a century later, coffee roasters were still trying to get it right. In Cairo, where there were more than one thousand coffee houses and plenty of people roasting coffee beans, only two people were roast gurus who knew how to roast properly in a mindful manner.

They attained this level of achievement by continually perfecting the process of what they were doing and being mindful by learning what did and didn't work to bring out the essence of the coffee bean.

Meditation is the same way. When you first begin to meditate, you'll find the way that will work best for you, through trial and error, until you find the perfect way—the method that suits you best and brings out the full flavor of your inner essence.

It will take you a lot less time than half a century to master the art of meditation. It can be easily achieved in the first five minutes, then you can roast your mindfulness to perfection to achieve the maximum flavor by fine-tuning meditation to fit your exact taste.

Today, roasting is a highly-evolved process that brings the essence of the coffee beans to life. As you mindfully meditate, you will bring the essence of your peaceful inner self into your life, into all your experiences.

The beans are poured into a preheated container and kept moving through a flow of hot air until they color evenly. As they warm up, the water inside them expands, turning into steam. As their inner structure is altered from the inside out, they make a cracking sound and begin to pop, almost like popcorn, opening slightly.

As you roast your inner essence and warm up to your meditation practice, you will begin to open your inner nature by changing the way you perceive things, probably jumping around a bit in your mind as you warm up to the full flavor of your inner essence.

After the first crack, the green coffee cherries turn color into a more vibrant green, then the color of straw, going into caramel and cinnamon, then to brown. Depending on how much longer they are roasted, the oils in the bean are brought forth and remain on the outside of the bean as a shimmery coating.

As you roast the essence of your inner nature from the inside out, you will bring forth the shimmers of your inner self and see them in all your experiences. At this point in the roasting process is where mastering the art of mindful meditation comes in. Roasted too much, the coffee beans will taste burned. Roasted a bit more and they will go up in flames. If you try too hard to meditate, your experience will have an unpleasant taste and you'll burn out.

By trying to achieve a Zen-like state of meditation by concentrating too much or overdoing it, you won't reach the simple serenity of the moment. Zen is simplicity. Zen is gentleness. Zen is harmony. Zen is balance. Zen breathes with you as you breathe with the essence of your inner self.

As you roast the flavor of your inner nature by mindfully meditating, you will be rewarded with the full flavor of the essence of the inner you.

During coffee roasting, the cracking noises diminish as the coffee beans smoke—as they prepare to release their inner essence—then the cracking noises start up again, this time with the wonderful aroma of freshly-roasted coffee as the beans achieve their full potential, as they reach perfection.

As you continue your meditation practice, you will achieve your full potential of being mindful as you release the full essence of your inner self.

After the coffee beans are roasted, they are often mixed together—customized and blended to bring out their subtle nuances and inner characteristics. Each bean from each coffee plant has a slightly different taste.

Each time you mindfully meditate will be slightly different as you customize your meditation, both to fit the situation you are in and to fit your lifestyle.

Coffee beans are selected and mixed to achieve the perfect blend of flavor. So it is with meditating. Through sampling various meditation mixes and discovering what works for you and how it works for you, you blend the knowing you've found and merge it together to create the custom blend of mindful meditation that shows you how to create the perfect cup of Zen coffee.

Chapter Six

Coffee, Coffee, Coffee

As you've discovered if you've begun meditating, and if you frequent coffee houses, coffee is so much more than coffee, just as there are so many ways to meditate. So many choices; so many coffees to choose from.

You have choices in the coffee you want in the same manner that you have choices in how and when to meditate. You choose the flavor of the coffee you want to experience. You choose the flavor of the meditation you want to experience and how you want to experience it.

You have endless choices and infinite variations, both with coffee and with meditation. You can create your own unique cup of coffee or specialty coffee drink with flavor shots to suit your taste and fit your style.

You can create your own unique style of meditation that suits your lifestyle and fits your personality by adding your individual tastes. You can find the essence of your inner self in your coffee by finding the best way for you to mindfully meditate.

While espresso is a drink unto itself, many coffee drinks are based on espresso. In Zen coffee, espresso is the same as the es-

50

sence of your inner nature—rich, deep, and powerful with a serene complexity. Since espresso is the basis for many coffee drinks, think of an espresso as the basis of your inner nature.

The word espresso is Italian in origin and means express. There are several meanings and applications of the word, just as in meditation, there are several levels and different applications of mindfulness.

Espresso is an express version of drip-brewed coffee; it takes 20 to 25 seconds instead of four to seven minutes to brew. Espresso is a concentrated, intense coffee. In many ways, it is the essence of coffee. Espresso is brewed through shots by forcing 200-degree water under intense pressure (140 pounds) through finely ground and lightly tamped coffee. This brings out the best in the coffee bean.

You don't have to meditate for hours to achieve enlightenment, to tune into the essence of your inner self. A small shot of mindfulness will bring out the intense, rich flavor of your inner essence. It will bring out the best in you in all your experiences.

The combination of pressure and precisely-heated water brings out the oils in the bean in a way that creates a smoother, more flavorful beverage than drip-brewed coffee. Oils in the bean are extracted and create the thick, full-bodied flavor and the tan upper layer called crema.

Crema is very aromatic and is the essence of the espresso shot. It shows the results of brewed espresso. The results you achieve by meditating show you how to bring out the crema of your inner nature.

An espresso grind is much finer than a drip-brew grind. By increasing the surface area of the bean through a finer grind, it takes less time to extract the right amount of soluble solids from the beans to brew the coffee. If you're short on time, you can increase your awareness to get into the essence of you. You can brew and blend your moments of mindfulness to extract the best from your meditations.

The grind for espresso is very important, just as the flow of mindfulness is important. If a coarse grind is used, it's like water running through rocks, producing a watery, dull espresso with no crema.

If the grind is too fine, it's similar to water moving slowly through sand, producing a thick, bitter crema. The water gets trapped inside the coffee grounds and turns into mud, producing a bitter espresso.

Neither grind produces a satisfying espresso or a satisfying meditation that brings out the essence of you. Somewhere in the center produces the perfect espresso shot and the most mindful meditation.

By centering within the essence of yourself, by simply breathing and being fully in the present moment, by going with the flow, you produce the perfect mindful meditation.

What is true of espresso is also true of meditating. With a coarse grind, the water will run right through without extracting enough of the coffee's essence, leaving no crema. Rushing through meditation, you won't extract the right amount of the essence of your inner self.

With a fine grind, the water will become trapped within the too finely ground coffee beans; it will flow slowly and turn to mud, with a very thick, bitter crema. A muddled mind will trap you within itself.

A perfect espresso shot will extract the right elements of the coffee bean and will have a rich, tan crema on top. A perfect mindful meditation will bring out the rich essence of your inner nature.

There are five steps in making the perfect espresso shot which are in harmony with the five steps in making the perfect mindful meditation.

☼ Purity of the water. The quality of the water is essential to the finished taste of espresso. The quality and pureness of your clear thoughts and intentions are essential to the flavor and outcome of your meditation.

☼ Grinding the beans to the proper grind—not too fine, not too coarse—is an important aspect of a perfect espresso. Finding the right method of meditating for you is an important aspect of mindful meditation. The correct grind of mindfulness occurs in centering yourself through your breath.

☼ Dosing is putting just the right amount of espresso into the brew basket to produce the perfect espresso shot. By giving your meditation the correct dose of attention and focus, you achieve the correct dose of mindfulness.

☼ Tamping refers to how firmly the espresso is packed in the brew basket before brewing. After putting in the proper dose of ground espresso beans, you tamp the espresso to even it out and lightly compact it so that the surface of the ground coffee is level and the water flows evenly and smoothly through it.

With mindful meditation, you smooth and even out your level of mind so that your mind is focused and mindfulness flows evenly and smoothly through it.

☼ Brewing the espresso shot is the final step that produces the end result; a perfect espresso with a perfect crema.

Brewing your meditation in a mindful manner produces the perfect shot of meditation which enables you to tune into your inner essence, the crema of your inner self.

There are four characteristics to look for in the perfect espresso shot, just as there are four characteristics to look for in the perfect mindful meditation:

☼ Essence. Crema should be tan, thick, smooth, and creamy; it should remain on the espresso for 60 to 90 seconds with a sweet lingering aftertaste. Mindfulness extracts the essence of your inner nature and remains with you.

☼ Time. Espresso is fast, taking 20 to 25 seconds. It doesn't take much time to meditate; 20 to 25 seconds to be mindful of your breathing and to be fully in the present moment is all you need.

☼ Volume. One shot of espresso is 1.5 ounces. The volume of your meditation will depend on what you put into it. Your meditation doesn't need to be long to be filled with the flavor of mindfulness; it only requires a short shot.

☼ Taste. A good espresso shot brings out the essence of the coffee bean; it tastes sweet and creamy, not bitter. Your mindful meditation brings out the full flavor of your inner essence, with a pleasant taste in your mind.

Just as in drip-brewing coffee, brewing the perfect espresso shot involves the purity of the water, the right amount of coffee beans, the correct grind, the proper level of ground coffee in the espresso brew basket, and the brew time.

Brewing the perfect cup of mindfulness is achieved by extracting your peaceful inner nature and allowing it to rise to the surface, to top your Zen coffee with the crema of your awareness.

More Zen, More Coffee

Zen is more than
a way to meditate.

It's a way of life, a way of
kindness and compassion.

Coffee is more than a drink.

It's a way to mindfully meditate, a
way to tune into your inner essence.

Chapter Seven

Zen Garden ~ Flowing in Harmony

Zen mindfulness—or meditating by coffee—expresses itself in a gentle frame of mind, a Zen peacefulness and harmony that flows naturally in and through your mind.

To achieve this state of mind, being in a Zen garden that is flowing in harmony can bring you into a perfect state of mindful meditation, into the true essence of your inner nature—just as the perfect espresso shot is topped with the essence of itself—crema.

Imagine you are in a peaceful Zen garden of serene simplicity. Within the garden are a few rocks placed on smooth sand. There is a fountain of water that originates from within the center of the carefully placed stones. The water gently gurgles and returns to the fountain—its essence—flowing in harmony.

Sitting in silence and listening to the gentle sound of flowing water brings you into a wonderful feeling of peacefulness. Just sitting quietly, mindfully listening to the gentle flow of water, you become aware of flowing smoothly into a serene state of mindfulness.

All is in balance and harmony. The water, the rocks, and the sand in the Zen garden within your mind bring you into a peaceful moment of mindfulness and combine to produce a perfect Zen meditation.

Now imagine the water you were so peacefully listening to has somehow become trapped and is no longer flowing smoothly. It has become a mere trickle of water that slowly meanders through the fine grind of coffee beans and spills onto the sand, turning it to mud. Something seems to be stuck, blocking the smooth flow and harmony of mindfulness.

Because you are mindfully meditating, you are aware that the water is wandering; it's somehow blocked and is not flowing in a natural, peaceful direction.

You liken this to a muddled mind—a mind that wanders during meditation, a mind that jumps all over the place, going in many separate directions at the same time, unfocused in its flow, getting stuck and muddled within itself, spilling into thoughts that distract you from the present moment. A muddled mind is not a focused mind which allows mindfulness to flow smoothly through it.

You move some of the stones to try to help the water flow peacefully and serenely along its mindful course again. The water begins to gush and flow too rapidly, trying too hard to achieve its natural flow.

It has not returned to a smooth flow of mindfulness; it has become a rapidly rushing waterfall gushing through the coarsely-ground coffee beans that produces the opposite of calm—not flowing into the essence of itself.

Pondering this for a moment, you become aware that when you try too hard to be mindful, to meditate, you are actually not flowing toward a peaceful moment; you are forcing the flow and trying to rush.

Wanting to return to a mindful state of peacefulness and harmony in the present moment, you bring your awareness into a calm, peaceful place within yourself to bring out the rich essence of your inner nature to produce a perfect meditation, flowing smoothly through the just-right grind of coffee beans that will produce the perfect mindful meditation.

You calmly breathe and become centered within the essence of yourself, simply being in the present moment, enjoying the flowing harmony of the Zen garden that is your mind—your inner essence.

Chapter Eight

Zen Coffee Choices

Once your espresso shot is made, you can take it in many different directions to make many different coffee drinks. Once you tune into the espresso of your essence, you can take your meditation in many different directions, depending on what you want to achieve from it.

You have endless choices and infinite variations with your choice of coffee drinks made to suit your taste, and with your individual flavor of meditating. You can create your own unique coffee drink to suit your style and fit your individuality and personality.

You can add any kind of flavor shots to your coffee and to your meditations to enhance the flavor of coffee and the flavor of mindfulness. A splash of happiness and calm included in your meditation can add joy and harmony to your life.

You can create your own flavor of meditating that suits your taste and fits your lifestyle by experimenting with various ways to mindfully meditate in all types of situations and experiences, as well as meditating by mindfully breathing, by silent sitting or purposeful walking, through visualization and imagery, and through focused awareness.

We naturally gravitate toward what we are most in tune with. It's the same with your choice of coffee drink and your choice of how to be mindful. You can mindfully meditate by tuning into your inner essence to find the way and style of meditation that will work best for you. You can match your flavor, taste, and personality with your choice of coffee.

Your coffee drink reflects the inner you and shows you your personality. Here's a coffee quiz in the form of a mindful meditation to show you what your coffee drink says about you and to give you insights into finding the best way for you to mindfully meditate.

Mindfully meditate on your choice of coffee drink. It's best to do this while you have your preferred coffee drink in hand. Breathe. Think about your coffee. Center in and focus on your coffee.

Intellectually, why do you like your coffee drink? What do you like about it? Why does the combination of flavors appeal to you?

Emotionally, how do you feel about your coffee drink? Why do you like the mix of ingredients in your coffee? Why do they appeal to you?

On both levels, how does your coffee drink reflect the inner you? Breathe and ponder this for a moment. What do the flavors you choose to add say about you? Breathe.

Ponder these things for a few mindful moments. Tune into your inner essence. Breathe. Let your thoughts be gentle on your mind.

Breathe. Take a slow drink of your coffee and savor it in your mouth for a moment before you swallow it. Mindfully taste and experience the unique flavors in your coffee, first separately, then simultaneously. Hear what the flavors say, listen to what they taste like.

What do your choices about the ingredients and flavors you add to the basic coffee show you? Breathe. Meditate on this for a moment; let the answer come gently into your awareness.

How does your coffee make you feel inside when you drink it? Breathe and ponder this.

What qualities does it both reflect and bring out in you? Breathe and ponder this.

How does the coffee and what you choose to add to it suit your personality and fit your lifestyle? Breathe.

Let your thoughts flow softly through your mind. Breathe. Let the intuitive awareness of your inner self speak to you as you listen softly in silence.

What you like about your coffee, what it says about you, and how you interpret it, will show you how to incorporate meditating into your lifestyle and to find the ways it will work for you because you'll be tuning into your inner nature and harmonizing your essence with the essence of your coffee.

Now that you know what your coffee says about you, you can mindfully meditate on your coffee—on the flavors and feelings you choose to add to your meditation—bringing out the essence of your inner qualities.

For example, if your drink is an iced vanilla latte with an extra shot, first think about how you describe your drink, keeping in mind that you are describing the essence of your personality.

Meditate on each part of the drink separately, then pull the combinations into harmony with one another.

Think about the coolness of the drink, the taste and the way it feels in your mouth and as you swallow it. Taste the flavor of the vanilla. Taste the extra espresso shot. Taste the creaminess of the milk.

Separate each flavor to taste its essence, then pull them all together into the whole experience of enjoying your Zen coffee in a mindful moment.

What does your coffee show you and what does it say about you? What do the individual items in your coffee drink show you about how to extract your inner essence into your experiences? What does your coffee tell you about how to blend meditation into your lifestyle?

A Cup of Morning Zen

The first cup of coffee in the morning
is a beautiful, enjoyable, Zen thing.

You're not quite awake and your mind is open
and receptive to the thoughts you drink in.

As you enjoy a cup of Zen coffee first thing
in the morning, allow the coffee to fill you with
a wonderful feeling of calm, peacefulness, and
harmony to set the tone of the day for you.

Chapter Nine

Wake Up and Smell the Coffee

Are you morning impaired? Coffee is the cure. Are you waking challenged? Coffee is the cure. Do you stumble out of bed with your eyes barely opened? Coffee is the cure. Do you need a shot of caffeine to jump-start your day and get you going? Coffee is obviously the cure.

Think your inner self is sleeping? Zen coffee is the cure. Think you don't have time to meditate? Zen coffee is the cure.

If you're like me first thing in the morning, all you can think about is having your coffee. In a way, this is a mindful meditation because the only thing on your mind is coffee.

To start your day off right, wake up and smell the coffee. Deeply breathe in the aroma and essence of your coffee to wake up your inner self first thing in the morning.

That's all you have to do. Breathe in the calm, peaceful essence of you. You may think that the calm, peaceful essence of you will put you back to sleep but this isn't true. This powers up your inner self like a shot of espresso wakes you up and gets you going.

If you're rushed in the morning, you can mindfully meditate in the time it takes you to enjoy a few quick sips of your coffee. If you have more than a few seconds, you can meditate for a moment or two as you slowly drink and savor your coffee.

Breathe in the aroma and essence of your coffee. Breathe in the flavor and essence of your inner self. Let yourself expand into the full aroma and flavor of both your coffee and your inner nature.

Luxuriate with your coffee for a few glorious moments to drink in the essence of your inner self to start your day off right. A mindful moment or two of drinking in your inner essence while drinking your coffee wakes you up to your inner self.

Maybe you need more than just breathing in your calm, peaceful essence by smelling the coffee or taking a few sips to wake you up to your inner nature. There are many ways to wake up your inner self, just as there are many tastes and inherent flavors in the character and qualities of coffee.

Maybe you need to breathe in some Zen eye-openers to begin your day in a calm, peaceful manner and to power up your inner self through the caffeine calm of Zen coffee.

One of the purposes of mindfully meditating is to use your breath to bring you completely into the present moment while you clear your mind of extraneous thoughts. But sometimes it's good to put a few thoughts in your mind. You can think and feel a morning mantra to wake up your inner self.

A mantra is a sacred word, chant, or sound that is used in meditation to aid you in becoming in tune with your inner nature—to become aware of your inner essence and to wake up your sleeping inner self.

By repeating the mantra, and being aware of the feelings it inspires and brings forth within you, you mindfully tune into the essence of the mantra to fill your mind completely in the present moment.

Just as the wonderfully rich aroma of your coffee is in the air, the richness of the flavors and feelings of your inner essence are in the air, wafting gently around, ready and waiting for you to breathe them in, to become mindful of them and own them as yours, to receive them as gifts from your inner self.

By breathing in words and the feelings associated with them, you achieve the same effect of being completely here now in the present moment. Drink in some Zen eye-openers while you're drinking your coffee.

As you breathe in the aroma of your coffee, simultaneously breathe in the Zen flavors and qualities of the essence of your inner nature. Breathe in all the wonderful feelings of happiness, health, harmony, peace, joy, calm, and love.

Breathe and be completely present with the feelings that are in tune with the inner essence of you. Feel the vibration of your mantra—the word and the feelings it brings forth—flowing within you and through you.

As you inhale the aroma, and drink your coffee in the morning, breathe in and drink the essence of the good feelings that are all around you and within you to wake up your inner self. Breathe in the essence of your Zen coffee. Breathe in the aroma and flavor of your inner essence.

Breathe in the aroma of your coffee; breathe in the flavor of your essence. Breathe out and be the flavors and feelings of happiness, health, harmony, peace, joy, calm, and love. Breathe in those feelings; breathe out those feelings.

☼ **Happiness**. Breathe in happiness. Breathe out sadness. Breathe. Happiness is in the air, gently floating all around you.

All you have to do is breathe it in. Breathe in the wonderful aroma, feeling, and flavor of happiness.

Breathe happiness in; feel it inside you. Feel it flowing within and through you; feel it within every part of your being—your essence. Breathe happy. Feel yourself becoming happy. Feel happiness resonating within you, vibrating in tune with the essence of you.

Breathe out unhappiness and despair. Let them go. Breathe in the essence and aroma of happiness; feel the taste and flavor of happiness gently flowing through you, filling you completely in the present moment.

Breathe in happy; completely be the feeling of happiness. Breathe in happy; breathe out happy. Breathe happiness. Breathe and be happy.

☼ **Health.** Breathe in health. Breathe out all the negative thoughts and feelings that are detrimental to your physical, mental, emotional, and spiritual well-being. Breathe. Health is in the air, gently floating all around you. All you have to do is breathe it in.

Breathe in the blessing aroma, feeling, and flavor of health. Breathe health in; feel it inside you. Feel it flowing within and through you; feel it within every part of your body, mind, and spirit, nourishing and rejuvenating you. Breathe health.

Feel yourself becoming healthy. Feel health resonating within you and flowing through you, vibrating in tune with the essence of you. Breathe out all your aches and pains and sickness. Let them go.

Breathe in the essence and aroma of health; feel the taste and flavor of health gently flowing through you, filling you completely in the present moment.

Breathe in health; completely be the feeling of health. Breathe in health; breathe out health. Breathe health. Breathe and be healthy.

☼ **Harmony**. Breathe in harmony; breathe out discord. Breathe. Harmony is in the air, gently floating all around you. All you have to do is breathe it in. Breathe in the delightful aroma, feeling, and flavor of harmony.

Breathe harmony in; feel it inside you. Feel it flowing within and through every part of you; feel it within your being—your essence. Breathe harmony. Feel yourself becoming harmonious. Feel harmony resonating within you, vibrating in tune with the essence of you. Breathe out conflicts and friction. Let them go.

Breathe in the essence and aroma of harmony; feel the taste and flavor of harmony gently flowing through you, filling you completely in the present moment.

Breathe in and completely be at one with the feeling of harmony. Breathe in harmony; breathe out harmony. Breathe harmony. Breathe and be in harmony with your peaceful inner essence.

☼ **Peace**. Breathe in peace. Breathe out anxiety and stress. Breathe. Peace is in the air, gently floating all around you. All you have to do is breathe it in. Breathe in the soothing aroma, feeling, and flavor of peace.

Breathe peace in; feel it inside you. Feel it flowing within and through every part of you; feel it within your being—your essence. Breathe peace. Feel yourself becoming peaceful.

Feel peace resonating within you, vibrating in tune with the essence of you. Breathe out all your cares and worries. Let them go. Breathe in the essence and aroma of peace; feel the taste and flavor of peace gently flowing through you, filling you completely in the present moment.

Breathe in peace; completely be the feeling of peace. Breathe in peace; breathe out peace. Breathe peace. Breathe and be peaceful.

✤ **Joy**. Breathe in joy. Breathe out sadness. Breathe. Joy is in the air, gently floating all around you. All you have to do is breathe it in. Breathe in the blissful aroma, feeling, and flavor of joy.

Breathe joy in; feel it inside you. Feel it flowing within and through every part of you; feel it within your being—your essence. Breathe joy. Feel yourself becoming joyful.

Feel joy resonating within you, vibrating in tune with the essence of you. Breathe out all your sorrows. Let them go. Breathe in the essence and aroma of joy; feel the taste and flavor of joy gently flowing through you, filling you completely in the present moment.

Breathe in joy; completely be the feeling of joy. Breathe in joy; breathe out joy. Breathe joy. Breathe and be joyful.

✤ **Calm**. Breathe in calm. Breathe out tension. Breathe. Calm is in the air, gently floating all around you. All you have to do is breathe it in. Breathe in the serene, tranquil aroma, feeling, and flavor of calm.

Breathe calm in; feel it inside you. Feel it flowing within and through every part of you; feel it within your being—your essence. Breathe calm. Feel yourself becoming calm.

Feel calm resonating within you, vibrating in tune with the essence of you. Breathe out all your problems and troubles. Let them go. Breathe in the essence and aroma of calm; feel the taste and flavor of calm gently flowing through you, filling you completely in the present moment.

Breathe in calm; completely be the feeling of calm. Breathe in calm; breathe out calm. Breathe calm. Breathe and be calm.

✭ **Love**. Breathe in love. Breathe out hate. Breathe. Love is in the air, gently floating all around you. All you have to do is breathe it in. Breathe in the beautiful aroma, feeling, and flavor of love.

Breathe love in; feel it inside you, inside your heart, mind, and soul. Feel it flowing within and through every part of you; feel it within your being—your essence. Breathe love. Feel yourself becoming filled with love.

Feel love resonating within you, vibrating in tune with the essence of you. Breathe out all your anger and resentments, all your woes and negativity. Let them go. Breathe in the essence and aroma of love; feel the taste and flavor of love gently flowing through you, filling you completely in the present moment.

Breathe in love; completely be the feeling of love. Breathe in love; breathe out love. Breathe love. Breathe and be love.

Breathe in the essence of your Zen coffee, and bring the essence of happiness, health, harmony, peace, joy, calm, and love with you wherever you go.

Where's Your Zen?

Is your Zen lost? Misplaced? Gone?
Does it only appear when you're feeling
calm and peaceful? Is it next to impossible
to find when you're stressed or angry?

Do you mindlessly gulp down your coffee
without giving Zen a second thought?
Not to worry. You're not alone.

All of us at one time or another have
misplaced our Zen. It isn't lost, though it
may have wandered off for a while, looking
for you in the moment when you lost your Zen.

Zen is everywhere, all the time.
Your Zen is hiding in your coffee and is
easily found when you look for it.
Wherever you go, there you are.

You can journey mindfully through life
with Zen coffee. Zen is flexible. Zen is fluid.

Zen fits your lifestyle. Zen is in every breath you take. Breathe and be present in the moment, no matter where you are, what you are doing, how you are feeling, or what is happening.

Breathe and be completely present with your feelings in the moment you are experiencing.

That's where your Zen is.

Chapter Ten

The Daily Grind

Now that you've had your morning cup of Zen coffee, it's time to put some peaceful, positive thoughts into your mind as you go about your day.

As you're breathing in the essence of your Zen coffee and your inner essence—vibrating in tune with all the good vibes of your inner self and radiating those qualities into the air around you—take a mindful moment to think nice, powerful thoughts to yourself. Think, feel, and/or say a few affirmations that you really like, ones you feel good about.

For example, think to yourself and really feel it, "Today is going to be a great day." No matter what you think the day will be like, set yourself up to enjoying and experiencing a great day, no matter what happens.

Put that thought and the feeling of it into your mind; be mindful of it all day. Breathe in the thought. Breathe out the thought. Be the thought. Breathe the thought. Let coffee be your reminder.

If your day throws some challenges your way or starts being not-so-great, simply take a mindful drink of your coffee or a nice, deep breath and remind yourself, "Today is a great day. I have Zen coffee. I am Zen coffee. Life is good. I'm good. Coffee is good." Breathe.

Depending on what is happening in your day, breathe and be the mantra of peace, joy, love, or whatever word-feeling is appropriate to your situation to turn your day around.

Here are a few more good thoughts and feelings that are in tune with the essence of you, ones that will keep your inner self awake and going strong all day.

Think to yourself and really feel it, "I feel wonderful. Great things are happening all around me and within me. I'm happy, healthy, and in harmony with myself. I feel peaceful. I feel the joy that is all around me and within me. I'm calm, both inwardly and outwardly. The essence of my inner self is love. I feel it all around me and within me, flowing through me and from me."

Breathe in those thoughts and feelings; breathe out those thoughts and feelings. Take a moment or two to be mindful of these wonderful thoughts and feelings you're putting into your mind and sending out all around you.

These mini mindful meditations are like drinking in a shot of espresso to power and flavor your day. Once you've had your morning coffee and breathed in your Zen eye-openers—and you and your inner self are completely awake—you can take your inner self with you when you leave the house.

Just as you can get your coffee to go, you can take your essence with you and mindfully drink it in all day. If your first stop before work or wherever you're going is the coffee house, you probably order your coffee with legs.

This means to go. Wherever you go, you can take the essence of your coffee and your peaceful inner nature with you. There's a saying in Zen Buddhism: Wherever you go, there you are.

But before you get there, you have to actually engage in the process of arriving. Your Zen coffee with legs has traveled with you into your car. You can mindfully experience your coffee as you drive to work and maneuver through traffic, even if you don't have a chance to drink it while driving.

Just be mindfully aware of your Zen coffee and your inner essence. Think peace. Breathe peace. Be peace. If ever there was a time for peacefulness with your awareness being completely in the present moment, it's when you're in your car driving through morning rush hour.

Drink in the peaceful essence of you; breathe in the essence of your Zen coffee in your car to keep you alert and focused. Breathe in the essence of peacefulness. Breathe out the essence of peace.

Breathe and be peaceful. With peace as your passenger, you'll arrive calmly at work or wherever you're going feeling peaceful and centered, not aggravated and scattered. Let peace be your driving mantra.

Engage the calm, peaceful essence of your Zen coffee in your mind as you're driving your car. Simply breathe in the presence of calm peacefulness, being completely aware and mindful in the present moment while driving your car, being completely alert and aware of the other cars on the road.

Be completely aware of all the interactions on the road between what other drivers are doing and how you are responding, between what you are doing and how other drivers are responding to your actions.

Breathe in the calm, peaceful essence of Zen coffee. Think peace. Breathe peace. Be peace.

If you find yourself getting stressed or upset by what other drivers are doing, simply think and feel the word peace in your mind. Repeat it to yourself as often as necessary. Breathe peace. Be filled with peace. Be peace.

Just as you travel mindfully in your car, you can travel mindfully through life with your Zen coffee.

Breathe and be present with your inner nature, the essence of who you are.

Zen Coffee Meditation

A Zen coffee meditation is something
you can do anywhere, anytime, with
or without coffee. All you need to do
is breathe and be mindfully present.

Chapter Eleven

Wherever You Go,
There is Zen Coffee

One of the purposes of mindful meditation is to be completely in the present moment to clear and still your mind so you can center into your inner essence. Another form of mindful meditation is walking meditation.

You already know your Zen coffee has legs and that your inner essence travels with you wherever you go. Walking slowly and peacefully with your complete attention on your steps brings you wholly into the here and now of the present moment.

Instead of running or quickly walking through your day—with cluttered thoughts running around taking their own steps in your mind—you can engage in a mindful walking meditation to get where you're going with the purpose of arriving at calm to reach a destination of peacefulness by focusing your thoughts on the process of walking.

A walking meditation is usually done outside in a calm, peaceful place in nature, following a path that leads you to a clearly-defined destination instead of just walking mindfully with no particular place to go. Being mindful of your steps and admiring and enjoying all that is around you and within you, you focus completely on what you see and feel in every moment.

You can revise walking meditation to fit the rhythm of your day. As you walk to wherever you need to go throughout the day, mindfully walk to get there. Focus and gather your thoughts for what you will do once you arrive. Bring your coffee with you or simply bring the essence of your Zen coffee with you. Step in rhythm with your essence.

Every now and then, stop for a mindful moment to take a sip of your Zen coffee and to breathe in the flavor of your essence. As you sip your coffee and breathe in the essence of your inner self, be aware that you are feeling calm, centered, and peaceful. Walk in a poetry of motion, a movement of harmony, a symphony of inner silence and peaceful solitude.

Walking meditation is done by walking slowly, purposefully, being completely aware and present in the moment, simply enjoying your steps that lead you into yourself, into the calmness and serenity of your inner self.

If you amble along with your thoughts simultaneously rambling, all you're achieving is a walk with steps that bring you outside yourself, not inside yourself to the calm place you want to arrive at.

If you find yourself walking with another emotion instead of peaceful calmness, mindfully tune into the emotion that is directing your steps and distracting your thoughts. Embrace that emotion and breathe into it. Let it flow through your mind.

Let your inner self make peace with it, then breathe it out, gently letting it go. Let the clear awareness of the emotion you are feeling bring you back into harmony, back into step with your inner essence, back into step with calm peacefulness.

Just as you step with peace, you can slurp the Zen of peacefulness. In the coffee industry, there is a procedure known as *cupping*. Roasters and other coffee cognoscenti [people in the know] come together to brew and taste the essence of various coffee beans to make the best coffee blends. This is done by smelling the coffee beans, grinding them, brewing the cup of coffee, and slurping the brewed coffee.

As you experience the activities that fill up your day, you will find yourself in situations where you can create the perfect cupping of your inner essence by creating your own mindful meditations to fit the situation you are in.

You can slurp in your calm, peaceful essence during the day to walk through the inevitable ups and downs of life to bring you completely into the present moment in any situation you find yourself in.

Wherever you go, there you are, with or without a cup of coffee in your hand. You can bring the essence of your calm inner nature into all your experiences.

Simply breathe in the aroma and flavor of Zen coffee; breathe in the aroma and flavor of your inner essence to bring you into a place of calm peacefulness in your mind.

You don't need to have coffee with you to breathe in your Zen coffee. The aroma and flavor of your peaceful inner essence is always with you, wherever you go. All you need to do is be awake and smell the coffee.

Mindfulness is Everywhere

You can find the mindfulness of Zen anywhere, at any time, no matter what you're doing or where you are.

You don't need to be a meditating monk on a mountain to achieve Zen or to sit in silence to listen to your inner spirit.

Whatever you're doing, wherever you are, is where you'll find mindfulness.

Chapter Twelve

Capturing the Calm
Within Your Coffee

Coffee starts your day off right, waking you up in the morning with a hot cup of java to open your eyes and get you going, as well as keeping you moving throughout the day and getting you through stressful situations in a peaceful manner. Throughout the day, you can tune into your peaceful, calm inner self by stirring your essence into your coffee.

Getting into the right frame of mind to meditate and tune into your inner essence may seem a bit elusive and next to impossible in your busy, hectic day. That may be the way it seems, but that's not the way it really is.

Even though you're running around, doing this, that, and the other, you can find many mindful moments during your day to meditate by centering yourself within the caffeine buzz to find peace and serenity wherever you go and whatever you're doing.

Every moment is a mindful opportunity to meditate, no matter where you are or what you are doing. You don't need to find a quiet place or a moment or two to meditate. Those moments will find you. Every moment can bring you into the present, into mindful awareness.

When you go within yourself to still your mind by meditating, you reach and touch the inner essence of who you truly are and you're in tune with the calm peacefulness of your inner nature. You can then bring that part of yourself into every aspect of your life.

Capturing the calm within your coffee is getting into the essence of you. Part of the paradox of mindfully meditating by coffee is to know when to let your thoughts go and when to listen to them.

Another part of the koan is capturing the calm. When you try to capture something, it implies that it's something elusive and that you're going to hold it prisoner once you obtain it. This doesn't work in mindful meditation.

You can't "capture" calm; the way to experience calm is to be in touch with your inner nature and be fully present in the moment. The calm comes in when you gently invite it into your mind. Simply allow yourself to experience calm in a welcoming atmosphere. Let it flow through you without trying to force it or hold on to it.

Meditation is a peaceful process; it can't be forced. If you don't feel like meditating or you're not feeling peaceful, then don't meditate. But maybe—and this is another paradox—maybe meditation is the direction you need to follow at this moment in time to bring you into peacefulness, to bring you into harmony with your inner nature.

Maybe a moment or two of mindfulness will put you in a peaceful frame of mind. Maybe all you need to do is tune in and turn on your coffee maker—your inner self that creates the calm, caffeine buzz in your life.

Chapter Thirteen

A Quiet Coffee Mind

The most widely known and commonly practiced form of Zen meditation is called sitting [zazen]. You sit on a cushion [zafu] on the floor with your legs folded in the lotus position, which can be a bit difficult to accomplish if you're not very flexible.

Your hands rest either on your lap or on your knees with palms opened upward. You sit quietly, clearing your mind of thoughts, cares, worries, and plans, letting go of both the past and the future, being only aware of the here and now of the present moment. You focus on your breathing, letting your breath bring you into the calmness and quiet of the present moment, into the gentle, peaceful essence of your inner nature.

When you find and/or make the time to enjoy a peaceful moment all to yourself—just you and a cup of coffee—and you've decided you're going to sit and mindfully meditate and be present in this moment of here and now, what usually happens? Your mind won't be quiet. A zillion thoughts rush and careen through your mind.

All you wanted was peace and quiet, a mindful moment of silence to sip your Zen coffee. Instead, you're listening to all the chatter running through your mind. This is called a monkey mind. Not too flattering, I know, but it happens to you when you meditate. Your mind goes in a zillion different directions at once, like a crazy little monkey jumping from one thought to another.

So how do you quiet your mind so you can focus on the present moment? By being accepting of your thoughts and being detached from them at the same time. Accept that thoughts are going to run through your mind, but don't become attached to them by thinking about them.

Calmly watch them come and go. Notice that you're having a thought, but don't pay attention to what the thought says. Without an audience, your thought will leave, and then another one will come running through your mind. Let the thought go, and the next one, and the next one, and so on.

Just breathe. Focus your mind on your breathing. Notice how you're breathing in and out, back and forth, inhaling and exhaling. Breathing in... breathing out. No room for thoughts, only breathing in and out. Just breathing, being present with your breath.

The zillion thoughts in your mind will leave you alone when you don't pay any attention to them. Your monkey mind wants attention; it wants an audience; it wants you to listen. When you simply notice that you're having a thought and don't focus on it, the thought will wander away by itself, wondering why you're not listening.

You're simply being mindful and breathing; you're capturing the calm within your Zen coffee. You're not listening to thoughts; you're listening to your breathing. Just breathe. Just be present with your breath.

Sitting meditation can be a paradox at times—a Zen koan. Many people think that sitting quietly without any thoughts is boring. Just as many people say it's quite enlightening, that calmly sitting brings quiet and clarity to your mind, along with the awareness of your inner nature.

At times, sitting quietly without allowing your thoughts to wander can seem like it's utterly worthless; you might tend to feel this way because your thoughts are wandering or because you have too many things to do, or there's too much on your mind.

At other times, sitting quietly to still your mind can prove to be valuable, calming you in stressful situations and allowing you to gather your wandering thoughts so you can think clearly.

If your thoughts go elsewhere while you're sitting, supposedly quietly meditating to still your mind and get into the peaceful essence of your inner nature, gently follow your thoughts to see where they lead you. They may lead you either in or out of your mind.

You can sit, either with or without thoughts, and with or without coffee, to capture your sometimes elusive inner essence. This can be easily accomplished while you're sitting at your desk at work or sitting in a comfortable chair at home.

You're sitting anyway, so why not incorporate a bit of mindfulness into it? This can ease tension and calm your mind. You don't have to contort your body into the lotus position. Simply sit comfortably with your back straight and your feet on the floor, hands resting gently on your lap.

Breathe in a feeling of peacefulness. Take a drink of your coffee or bring to mind the aroma and flavor of your coffee to center yourself within the caffeine buzz to tune into the essence of your inner nature. Breathe.

Mindfully meditate on your coffee or on the qualities of your coffee. Breathe. Focus and center in on the Zen of your coffee.

Breathe. Focus and center in on the calm essence of your inner nature. Breathe.

Let all your thoughts gently flow out of your mind. Just let them go. Breathe in calm peacefulness. Breathe out worries and tension. Breathe in the essence of Zen coffee. Let your mind gently float into the ethereal essence of the steam rising from your hot coffee. Breathe.

Let your mind softly flow into the ethereal essence of you. Breathe in the Zen. That's all you have to do; just meditate on your coffee and breathe while you're sitting to drink in and enjoy the calm essence of your inner self.

There are many ways to mindfully meditate; sitting is one of them. Some people feel that sitting is too rigid and uncomfortable. Others feel that sitting helps you transcend your physical nature, rising into the ethereal essence of your spiritual nature, just like the steam rising from your hot cup of coffee.

Any meditation you engage in should feel good, be comfortable, relaxing, nurture your mind, nourish your soul, and fit easily into your lifestyle.

Zen Stillness

Be still.
Breathe in the stillness.
Be the stillness.

Listen.
Breathe in the silence.
Be the silence.

Let your thoughts float on
the wind, as soft and silent
as a whisper of the wind.

Listen to the whispers of silence.
Be the whisper of stillness.
Listen to the stillness of silence.

Be. Breathe. Zen.

Chapter Fourteen

Being Here, Now

Watch your wandering thoughts to bring you into the present moment, the moment of here, now. Another form of sitting meditation that isn't as structured as zazen is something you've done many times before. It's called visualization or inner imagery and is also known as daydreaming.

How often have you zoned out during a dull business meeting, or were waiting in a doctor's office or sitting in a car repair shop waiting for your car to be fixed, and your thoughts wandered to more pleasant things?

How many times have you been sitting at your desk at work, staring out the window while your thoughts traveled outside of your immediate environment?

While your thoughts wandered during a daydream, they were also focused. You were mindfully meditating; you were completely present and mindful of the scenes inside your mind.

You can add another dimension to mindfully meditating; you can introduce focused awareness through inner imagery and visualization to capture both the calm and the caffeine within your coffee.

Daydreaming is a wonderful way to mindfully meditate, to place your thoughts into a pleasant place somewhere outside yourself to bring you into the peaceful, calm essence of yourself. Have you ever noticed how peaceful, calm, and relaxed you feel when you're in a beautiful garden or when you're at a beach on a beautiful sunny day, listening to the motion of the waves as they gently ebb and flow?

You can place your awareness into the serenity of nature to invite peacefulness into your mind and to tune into your inner nature. If you'd rather be at the beach instead of at work, here's a mindful focused awareness meditation you can do while sitting at your desk.

Take a deep breath in. As you let it out slowly, imagine that your breath is like the ocean with the waves coming and going, matching the rhythm of your breath as you inhale and exhale.

As the waves ebb and flow, you breathe in and out. Breathe with the essence of your inner self. Breathe with the gentle ebb and flow of the ocean.

Listen to the waves as they come up to the shore; watch them as they recede into the ocean. Watch the gentle motion of the waves as you breathe in and out, as the waves ebb and flow.

Breathe in and out, in a natural rhythm and flow that is in harmony with the tides, in harmony with the essence of your calm, peaceful inner self. You're just breathing and being, breathing and listening to the sound of the waves as they flow in a natural rhythm and harmony.

You feel perfectly peaceful as you breathe in rhythm and harmony with the calm essence of your inner self, as you breathe in rhythm and harmony with your inner nature.

Your mind is free and uncluttered, in harmony with the present moment of here and now.

Listen to the harmony that is all around you and within you. Breathe in the harmony of the essence of your inner self. Be in tune with and mindful of the rhythm and harmony of your breathing.

Listen to the waves of the ocean breathing in rhythm and harmony with the essence of you. Feel the breath of your inner self mindfully breathing inside you as you breathe in and out.

Listen to the rhythm and harmony of your mind, in tune with the natural, peaceful essence of you. Just breathe and be for a few moments.

Chapter Fifteen

There's No Time Like the Present

The essence of your inner self is right here, right now, completely in the present moment. While daydreaming can bring you into the present moment in a focused meditation, there are times when daydreaming takes you somewhere other than the present.

If your thoughts are traveling in the past or the future, you're not in the present moment. The present moment is where you find the peaceful essence of yourself.

Perhaps you're thinking about something nice you want to have happen or worrying about something bad you think might happen, or you're stressing about or regretting something that has already happened.

A mantra that you might like to silently repeat to yourself when your thoughts are going into the future in anticipation of something that may or may not happen, is to tell yourself, "I'm not there yet; I'm here now." Breathe.

If your thoughts are going into the past, tell yourself, "Been there. Done that. I'm here now." Breathe. These few words, along with your breath, will return you to the present moment.

You can capture the calm essence of your inner self and bring that calmness into all your experiences. Every situation you're involved in provides you with avenues to mindfully meditate.

All the ordinary, routine, aggravating, and sometimes irritating activities like grocery shopping, getting gas, waiting at the doctor's office, and other situations that are utterly boring can turn into wonderful, mindful experiences that bring you into the present moment.

Meditation may be the farthest thing from your mind when you're standing in line at the grocery store waiting to check out. This is one of those mindful moments that find you.

You can choose to be aggravated because the person in front of you is taking way too long to dig around in her purse to find her checkbook or you can choose to take this moment to calmly and mindfully breathe in the essence of Zen coffee, to breathe in the peaceful essence of your inner nature.

Simply breathe and focus on your breathing. Be aware of where you are right here and now. Be present in the moment. Listen to the thoughts and feelings that come into your mind. Center yourself into the situation. Be there, fully, with your attention and focus.

You're in the grocery store so maybe you'd like to mindfully meditate on the food that is in your grocery cart or perhaps you'll choose to simply breathe and be, to be calm and peaceful, mindfully aware of the essence of your inner nature.

Instead of worrying about the high price of gas or where you need to go next, take these moments at the gas station to be mindful of the calm essence of your inner self.

If you want to let thoughts run through your mind, perhaps you'd like to think about how the gas powers your car, just as breathing powers your body, and how coffee gives you energy, or maybe you'd like to take these moments to go quietly within yourself, to breathe in rhythm and harmony with your peaceful inner essence.

While waiting in the doctor's office, or at the car repair shop, or anywhere else, we often try to find things to distract us from the experience of simply waiting. This is a perfect time to breathe in the essence of your inner nature, to take some time to breathe and be mindfully aware that you're breathing.

Take this time to simply be in tune with your Zen nature. By simply breathing and being aware that you're breathing, you'll be here, now, completely in the present moment—in the peaceful present moment of simply being—enjoying the calm essence of your inner self.

Another seemingly boring situation is washing the dishes or rinsing them and putting them into the dishwasher. Instead of rushing through this, especially if washing the dishes is unpleasant for you, take this time to focus your full awareness on what you are doing.

Completely immerse yourself in this experience of washing the dishes. Feel the temperature and the sensation of the water on your hands. Feel the silky smoothness of the soap. Notice the bubbles. Be aware of the scent of the soap. Mindfully be aware of the process you are engaging in as you wash the dishes.

You can capture the calm within your coffee and find the mindfulness of Zen anywhere, anytime, all the time, and in any situation—while drinking coffee, being in a beautiful garden, washing the dishes, mowing the lawn, writing a book, cooking dinner, painting a picture, walking through the rain, grocery shopping, riding a motorcycle, dancing, playing with your dog, cuddling with your cat, running or jogging, and taking out the trash.

Mindful moments are everywhere and are happening all the time. All you have to do is recognize them to capture the calm essence of Zen coffee, to capture the calm essence of your inner self. Capturing the calm within your coffee is simply being fully in the present moment and being mindfully aware of what you are doing.

Mindfully meditating is an attitude you are completely in charge of. Mindfully meditating in any situation you are in is a choice. It's been said that attitude is everything, that the attitude you have and embrace governs how you experience all the activities and events in your life.

In Zen, an attitude of gratitude is mindfully cultivated and all experiences are viewed as sacred.

Instead of being aggravated while waiting in line at the grocery store, be grateful for the food you are buying. While filling your car with gas, be grateful you have a car that will take you where you want and need to go. Focus your awareness on these things.

Instead of feeling impatient or bored while waiting for an appointment, instead feel thankful you have given yourself this opportunity to meditate, to mindfully tune into the essence of you to achieve the calmness that is within you.

Your peaceful essence is always with you and available to you in every moment. You can choose to embrace it and mindfully engage your awareness.

Whatever you're doing, wherever you are, and whatever is happening, is where you'll find the calm within your Zen coffee.

The Present is a Gift

In every moment, you have a new beginning.
The present moment is always a gift. You always
have an ever-present choice to tune into your
spiritual essence, to tune into your Zen nature, to
take the present moment to mindfully meditate.

You can take any moment you wish and turn it into
a present Zen moment, with or without coffee.

Being present in every moment is a gift
you give yourself. A gift that brings you peace,
joy, calmness, and harmony. A gift that offers
you the opportunity to just simply be and
breathe, a present that gives you the chance
to tune into yourself and your inner essence.

Chapter Sixteen

Coffee Zendo

Alone at last; peace and quiet. A breather, a coffee break; just you and your coffee. You can enjoy a state of mind where you experience calm, peace, joy, and harmony simply by going within yourself to drink in the essence of your inner nature.

You can find a few moments every now and then during your day to peacefully meditate and become mindful of who you really are, to tune into your inner nature.

If you think you can't find a few moments, then just drink your coffee mindfully, being aware that the caffeine in your coffee gives you the pizzazz and power to create a calm Zen state of mind, a meditative space, a coffee sanctuary for a few moments of meditation every day no matter where you are, what you are doing, or what is happening around you.

This is also part of the koan of meditating by coffee—allowing the caffeine in your coffee to calm your mind and bring you into a meditative, mindful frame of awareness.

While you can meditate anywhere, anytime—emptying your mind of stressful thoughts by focusing on your Zen coffee and the gentle awareness of your inner self—sometimes it's easier to meditate if you create the space in your mind to experience Zen tranquility.

In the outer world of Zen, this place is called a zendo; it's a meditation hall where it is peaceful and quiet; a serene place to meditate; a place to quietly sit in mindful meditation.

In the inner world of your mind, this place is called an inner sanctuary; it's a state of mind and a frame of awareness—a place to tune into the essence of your inner nature.

Zen coffee has its own version of a zendo. Let your coffee break be your zendo—wherever you are.

Begin your coffee break before your actual coffee break. Imagine the coffee, the time alone, the time to tune into the peaceful essence of your inner nature, and the time to simply enjoy silence. This is a mindful meditation in itself.

While looking forward to the coffee break you'll be enjoying later, begin with an attitude of gratitude. An immediate thought that may run through your mind is, "Oh, thank God I'm going to have a coffee break in 30 minutes!"

Or you may begin to simply feel a sense of the calm peaceful-ness you'll be experiencing when you have your Zen coffee break.

When your coffee break actually happens, go for solitude. This is not the time to chat or call a friend to meet you.

This is the time to still the chatter going on inside your mind, to let go of the stresses that may have built up during your day for a few glorious moments of peace and quiet.

Find an empty table in the break room, or at the coffee house, or wherever you are having your coffee. It doesn't matter how busy it is, how many people are there, who is talking about what on their cell phone, or any other distractions. This is only about you and your Zen coffee; that is all there is for these few mindful moments you gift yourself with during the day.

Give yourself a few minutes to relax and tune into your inner nature. Let your Zen coffee transport you into a peaceful place of silence within you. Sitting by yourself, pick up your coffee cup and hold it in your hands for a moment to experience the feel and sensation of your coffee cup.

Put your hand around the cup and feel its warmth. Focus on this feeling. What does it feel like as the warmth permeates your hand and begins to spread through you, warming you with the thought of a quiet coffee and some peaceful time alone?

Bring your attention to the sensation of warmth in your hand and notice—just simply notice the warmth. Nothing more, nothing less. Thoughts and worries may rush into your mind, crowding each other to get your attention. The seemingly endless stream and barrage of words, thoughts, cares, worries, and plans is your monkey mind at work.

Focus only on your feelings that the warmth of the cup brings forth in you. This will help you clear out the clutter from your mind. The whole idea of this Zen coffee break is to achieve stillness and inner peace.

Sometimes, maybe most of the time, you have to let your thoughts run rampant through your mind without pondering them. Just watch your mind go through its motions and maneuverings while moving toward inner stillness and peace.

Smell the coffee; breathe in the aroma. Focus only on the aroma; let the aroma of your coffee be your point of reference. Nothing else matters, nothing else is important. This is your time for you and Zen coffee.

You can feel your awareness entering into a calm place of stillness and peace within you. Let yourself relax into the aroma of your coffee; relax into the calm essence of your inner self. Don't force the feeling. Just simply let it happen.

Take a drink of your coffee. Notice the feel of the warmth on your lips, your tongue, and the taste of the coffee in your entire mouth before you swallow.

Really pay attention to the taste of your coffee. Focus on the taste. Be present to the feelings you have as you sip your coffee and feel its warmth flowing through you.

Breathe. Take a few deep, long breaths. Notice yourself having a sip, swallowing, and then sitting back with a long, slow inhalation and slow, thought-less exhalation. Repeat this three or four times before enjoying your next sip.

It's just you and your coffee. It's just you and stillness. It's just you, breathing and being with your Zen coffee. It's just you, experiencing peace.

With the stillness comes silence—maybe not all around you, but within you, and this is where the silence whispers gently into and through you, through the mindful awareness of your Zen coffee.

This is your time to quiet yourself. This is your time to simply be quiet, to simply feel peaceful. This is your time to experience the quiet stillness and silence within you.

Let your mind drift into peace. Let your mind experience stillness and silence. Breathe.

When your coffee break is over and you return to work or whatever you are doing, you will feel wonderfully relaxed and refreshed, filled with the calm, peaceful essence of your inner self and your Zen coffee.

End your coffee break the same way you began—with an attitude of gratitude, feeling thankful for what you have just felt and experienced with your Zen coffee break.

Chapter Seventeen

Zen Sanctuary

While you can experience the tranquility of a zendo anywhere, Zen is most evident in a peaceful place in nature—a garden. Simply being in a garden can bring you into mindful awareness, with or without your Zen coffee.

A Zen garden captures the simple essence and serenity of nature, bringing you into harmony with your inner self and your environment.

You can focus your awareness within yourself, within a Zen sanctuary, a zendo coffee garden, by creating a calm, peaceful place in your mind where you can reconnect with yourself on an inner level to savor the taste and enjoy the full flavor and pure essence of your inner nature.

The nature of coffee is similar to your inner nature. Coffee is simplicity by its very nature; a cup of coffee originates from a coffee bean. Coffee is in harmony with nature; coffee beans and water are all that's needed to create a cup of coffee, to bring the essence of the bean into a cup of Zen coffee.

The nature of your inner essence is divine simplicity; your inner nature is peaceful and in harmony with everything. All that's needed to create a mindful moment is the desire to create that moment of mindfulness within yourself.

Your Zen sanctuary is a state of mind and a coffee frame of awareness; it's a beautiful garden where you simply enjoy the serenity of your inner nature, the Zen essence of your inner self. It's a place where you feel connected and in harmony with yourself.

A Zen garden is a simple, pleasing, healing, renewing space; it's where you nurture yourself, where you breathe in the freshness and clarity of the pure essence of your inner self. A Zen garden is soothing and simple, in harmony with the peaceful tranquility of your inner self.

Breathe. Imagine you're in a beautiful, serene, tranquil place, a Zen coffee garden. Breathe in the aroma of coffee, the fresh air, and the jasmine-scented fragrance of this peaceful sanctuary; breathe in the essence of your inner self. Focus your awareness into a Zen garden within your mind.

Your Zen sanctuary might be high on a mountain where coffee grows best in the higher altitude, where your inner self grows best in the higher altitude of your mind. Your Zen garden might be an open area—simple and pleasing—with a few rocks and some coffee plants; perhaps a gently flowing stream of water is softly rippling through your peaceful Zen sanctuary.

Your Zen garden is whatever you picture in your mind that brings you into a place of peace and harmony within yourself. Your Zen sanctuary is where you feel most in tune with your inner nature.

Breathe. Create your Zen garden—your inner sanctuary—in your mind. Imagine it and bring the images of your thoughts into a Zen sanctuary where you feel most peaceful and in tune with yourself, in tune with your inner nature.

Picture your Zen garden inside your mind and be there. Be there in your Zen sanctuary in your mind. Breathe in the peacefulness and serenity of your Zen coffee sanctuary. Just breathe and be there.

Breathe in the ambience and aura of peacefulness and serenity. Breathe in the clear freshness and pure simplicity of your Zen coffee garden. Breathe in the peacefulness of your Zen sanctuary as you allow this space—this coffee frame of mind to nurture your inner self and nourish your mind. Breathe.

Feel the calm peacefulness and serenity of your Zen sanctuary flowing through you, renewing you and nourishing you. Breathe in the beauty and joy and harmony of your Zen space. Breathe out the stresses and tensions of your day. Let them go.

Simply breathe and be in the beauty and serenity of your peaceful Zen sanctuary within you. Let the tranquil essence of your Zen garden surround you and flow through you.

Just breathe and be in your Zen sanctuary for a few mindful moments, being completely present in the here and now of your Zen sanctuary.

You can create this Zen space—this coffee frame of mind—whenever you want to, wherever you are, whatever you are doing, and whatever is happening around you.

Within your Zen garden, you can tune into your inner nature by tuning into the essence of your inner self. Your Zen garden—your coffee sanctuary—is where you're in harmony with your inner nature, where you're in tune with the qualities of your natural essence—happiness, health, harmony, peace, joy, calm, and love.

Flowing into Zen

The path of Zen is gentle,
peaceful, and flows like water,
following its own course.

Zen coffee is simply
going with the flow of life,
in harmony with all of life.

Chapter Eighteen

The Koan of Coffee

You have a dual nature—your inner nature that you're aware of by mindfully meditating and your outer worldly nature which you experience in your daily activities. Both are twins of one another, seeming opposites that you can bring into harmony.

The purpose of mindful meditation is to bring out the essence of your inner self into all your everyday activities and experiences, to blend them into a unified whole, just as the purpose of coffee is to bring out the essence of the bean, to blend the bean's inherent qualities into a perfect cup of coffee.

By viewing the world—both the outer world of the experiences in your life and the inner world of your meditation that you experience in your mind—as a whole, a combination of all the parts of you—your thoughts, feelings, and experiences—you see the totality of your essence, the completeness of who you are.

In your mind, in your Zen sanctuary, you can be completely in tune with who you are. You can relax and be natural, in harmony with your essence.

As you go out into the world—to work, to run errands, to do whatever you do—you tend to separate the wholeness of yourself into the many roles you have. By being mindful, you can bring the seeming separateness of yourself into the wholeness of all your thoughts, feelings, and experiences.

This is what the Zen of coffee is all about—combining your inner qualities with your outer experiences, blending them into a unified, completely mindful experience—whatever you are doing, wherever you are, and whatever is happening.

Be in your peaceful Zen garden—your coffee sanctuary to ponder the koan of meditating by coffee. As you're breathing in harmony with your inner self, breathing in harmony with the peaceful serenity of your inner sanctuary, you notice a beautiful coffee tree growing in your Zen garden. Your coffee tree looks like a shrub; it has long skinny branches with shiny green leaves.

You see tiny, delicate, jasmine-scented blossoms and clusters of green and rosy ripe berries growing simultaneously together. Even though you can't see it, you know that inside each berry are two coffee beans nestled together in harmony—twins of the same nature.

Imagine your inner self as a beautiful, resilient coffee tree, grounded in the earth and reaching for the light of the sun in the sky, the essence of your inner self growing in harmony with both the earth and the universe.

Feel yourself grounded in your physical world while simultaneously feeling your essence growing free and natural, blessed with the abundant richness of the earth and nourished by the unlimited resources of the universe.

Just as the branches and leaves of your coffee tree reach for the light of the sun, you reach higher into the light of your inner self, gently stretching your mind, reaching for the light within you. Watch your inner self growing, stretching, reaching for the light. Breathe in the essence of who you are, receiving nourishment from both the earth and the universe. Breathe out the essence of who you are, sharing your essence with both the earth and the universe.

This is the basis of all forms of meditation—being grounded while simultaneously reaching to attain enlightenment, peace, harmony, and joy, and to incorporate that peaceful essence into every part of your life.

In your mind—your imagination—go within the coffee tree, within yourself, into the two coffee beans. Be aware of the coffee beans growing together in harmony. Be aware of your inner self and your physical self growing together in harmony.

See the dual nature of your essence; be aware of both the harmony and the separateness. Breathe. Blend these two parts of yourself into a unified whole, breathing and being in harmony with these parts of yourself.

This is also part of meditation, to bring your inner awareness out into all your experiences, where you can use what you've gained from your meditation in a practical manner.

Mindfully meditate on your coffee tree; send it love vibes. Feel the love radiating out from your inner self to your coffee tree. Send love vibes to yourself and receive love vibes from your inner self. Feel the love radiating from your Zen coffee tree into your inner self.

Feel the love in your inner self radiating out into the world around you. Breathe and feel the love. Be aware of the harmony that is all around you and within you.

Breathe the fresh, coffee-scented air in your Zen garden. Breathe in the wonderful aroma and flavor and essence of your Zen coffee garden inside your mind.

Breathe in the gentle, jasmine-scented fragrant breeze from the coffee cherries growing on the coffee tree in your Zen garden; feel the scent wafting through your inner self. Breathe in the freshness of the air that is filled with the Zen of peacefulness.

Feel the gentle, calm breeze encircle your body and fill your mind. Feel the soft caress of its touch. Breathe in the gentle breeze that is softly scented with coffee and jasmine. Breathe in the calm, gentle essence of your inner self.

Feel the peaceful breeze flowing softly through you, cleansing your mind and spirit, healing and refreshing you. Breathe out the clearing breeze, letting it gently blow away all your cares and worries. Let them go, let them disappear softly into the air.

Breathe in the gentle, calm breeze of your Zen sanctuary. Breathe in the peaceful, breezy essence of your inner self. Let the calm breeze softly surround you, encircling you and filling you with peace of mind.

Breathe and be with the calm breeze, with the peaceful essence of your inner nature. Breathe and be in your inner sanctuary—your Zen coffee garden. Breathe.

You can bring the qualities of your inner self forth in your life whenever you want to, wherever you are, whatever you are doing, and whatever is happening around you. You can find a few mindful moments every day to be in your Zen sanctuary, to tune into your inner nature, and drink in the good vibrations of Zen coffee.

It's been said that Zen is essentially a state of mind or spirit that permeates all of life. Mindfully meditating originates from within you and brings out the essence of your inner self into every part of your life.

The paradox of meditating by coffee is that mindfully meditating is not separate from any of the experiences in your life; it is a basic, integral part of everything in your life and can be incorporated into every thought, feeling, and experience you have, much in the same manner that caffeine and calm—which are seeming opposites—poured into the same coffee cup are a perfect blend of meditation and mindfulness.

Your coffee zendo, your Zen sanctuary, and your coffee garden, while being an inner place to mindfully meditate, is also a place of mind in real life where you actively engage in mindfulness in and through all your activities.

You can allow the experiences in your day to bring you into your Zen sanctuary, into mindful awareness by embracing the coffee cup of life.

The Zen Zone

Are you in the Zen zone?

Being in the zone means you're totally in tune with whatever you're doing, whether it's drinking coffee, simply breathing, admiring a beautiful flower, cleaning your house, meditating, enjoying a sunrise, swimming at the beach, jogging, reading, or anything else you do.

The nature of Zen is in harmony with everything and everything is in harmony with Zen.

You can be in the Zen zone in every moment.

Simply allow yourself to flow into whatever you're doing with your full focus of awareness.

Chapter Nineteen

The Coffee Cup of Life

How do you mindfully meditate through all of life's ups and downs? What do you do when life throws you a curve or distracts you sideways? How can you center into the calm, peaceful essence of your inner self when you're totally involved in the throes of life?

The answer is to drink fully of your Zen coffee, to just simply be there with your coffee, to mindfully be with every situation and experience in your life. Be fully engaged and mindfully present.

Embrace the coffee cup of life with all its flavors and complexities, its ups and downs, its nuances and overtones, qualities and characteristics. Breathe. Be involved in what you are feeling, thinking, and experiencing.

The nature of coffee is in tune with and in harmony with its environment. It is present in every moment, going with the flow, growing into the essence of itself. As the beans share their essence with you in your coffee, they remind you of your inner essence and how you can be in tune with and in harmony with your environment.

Coffee can show you your Zen nature. Coffee helps you to be present in every moment, to go with the flow of whatever is happening, to be mindfully present and engaged, and to grow into your inner essence.

Every coffee bean is individual and unique, with its own personality and unique flavor. The one thing they all have in common is that the inherent nature of coffee beans is Zen.

Growing in a Zen-like state of mindfulness and harmony, the little beans dream of becoming lattes or espressos, cappuccinos or mochas. Every bean's sole purpose is to bring you the best cup of coffee it can, to blend themselves in harmony with the coffee cup they find themselves in.

The qualities of coffee beans are Zen-like in their natural essence, mindfully meditating to bring forth their individual flavors. Some beans are hearty and robust, others have an earthy complexity with a hint of nuttiness, some are smooth and mellow. Other beans are smoky and rich, some have overtones of floral aromas and fruitiness, while others offer a soft spiciness with hues of rich cinnamon.

Some are deeply intense and flavorful, some are complex with a gentle stroke of silkiness, and some are vibrant with a delicate sweetness. Some beans are strong and fragrant, others offer a pure, syrupy richness with sweet hints and soft undertones of deep flavors.

Every coffee bean has its own essence and personality, just as every situation you're in is flavored with overtones and hues of meaning, and brings forth various nuances of feelings, allowing you to extract what you want to achieve in the situation as you mindfully brew the flavors of what you are experiencing.

Since life, and the nature of Zen, is filled with surprises and paradoxes, there are peaberry coffee beans, which are very individual and deeply in harmony with themselves. Perhaps we should consider the peaberry to be an enlightened coffee bean; having attained harmony with its duality, it is one with itself.

Usually, there are two flat green coffee beans inside a coffee cherry, growing together in harmony, yet each has its own qualities and characteristics. But occasionally, the bean has a mind of its own and decides to be at one with its inner nature and only one football-shaped bean develops.

This single bean is called a peaberry. It has no dual nature; it is complete within itself. It has achieved, by its own choice, a Zen harmony with itself which has its own distinctive taste and flavor, essence and quality.

Just as each bean, whether it's a twin by its dual nature or a peaberry by its harmonious nature, has its own characteristics and qualities which are reflected in your cup of coffee—you, too, have a myriad complexity of characteristics and qualities within you which are reflected in your response to everything that occurs in your life.

You can make every experience in your life a Zen cup of coffee as you minimize stress and maximize happiness. You can find Zen in quiet hidden places in your mind where you never thought to look for them.

Finding peace, quiet, and harmony within yourself, within the essence of your inner self is achieved by being mindfully present in every situation and focusing on the qualities of your inner nature, on the essence of the coffee bean you feel most in tune with.

No matter where you are or what you are doing, Zen coffee is there, too.

Chapter Twenty

The Caffeine of Calm

Drinking coffee when you're in a stressful situation allows you to gather your thoughts to be mindfully present. As you drink your coffee, allow the coffee to calm and clear your mind. Allow the calm within the caffeine to focus your thoughts and feelings. Let the caffeine calm of your Zen coffee fill you with the peaceful essence of your inner nature.

How do you take your coffee? Do you lighten it up with cream and sugar for sweetness? Do you like it strong and black or do you prefer a creamy latte? Is decaf your style? How do you react to the situations and stresses in your life?

Do you prefer a light roast or a dark roast? Do you look on the lighter side of situations or do you look at the darker side? Lighter roasts are livelier, laced with subtleties and sweet nuances. Darker roasts are rich and velvety, grounded in heavier tones and smoky hints.

Roasting the beans brings out each bean's most flavorful and distinctive characteristics. Part of the bean's journey into your coffee cup consists of being true to its inner nature. When roasted to the peak of its perfection, it brings out the inner qualities and characteristics of itself, sharing the full essence of its inner nature.

After the beans are roasted, they are ground to produce the perfect cup of coffee. You can grind your own beans to make every experience in your life a Zen cup of coffee by processing mindfully before expressing what's on your mind. Take a peaceful Zen moment to meditate on your coffee and to roast the flavors of your feelings before you say anything or act on your emotions.

Just as the correct grind is important for both brewed coffee and espresso, so the just-right grind is needed in every experience to extract the right elements from the situation and brew the perfect solution or the right manner in which to approach and engage in the situation.

But before the grind comes the bean. What's the characteristic of the bean you identify with in each situation and experience in your life? What flavor do you want to extract from the bean and from the situation? How do you want to roast the flavors, then brew the grind?

It all begins with the bean, with the flavor of the situation you are in and how you choose to respond to it. What you experience with your coffee, and with your life, depends on the bean you choose to put into your coffee and the way you choose to experience what occurs in your life.

Zen is the way of balance, the way of peace and harmony. The subtle nuances and similarities between the coffee beans and mindfulness combine and lend themselves to a cup of Zen coffee.

You can do a mindful meditation on the situation you're in to achieve the perfect Zen cup of coffee. Be the coffee beans of negative and positive; be aware of your dual nature and both sides of the situation. Blend the beans. The purpose of the duality of your nature is to bring you into balance with yourself.

Honor the essence of the bean; honor your feelings. Be true to yourself, to your inner nature.

You can create your own unique mindful meditations—your own custom blend of Zen coffee—to fit every experience you have by being mindful of and accepting what you're feeling in the present moment of here and now, to extract the full flavor from the coffee beans of the situation.

You can flavor your meditations with your inner essence to brew your experiences in a mindful manner. For example, when you're at the grocery store waiting in a long, seemingly never-ending line, you're probably feeling a bit impatient.

The nature of Zen coffee is to achieve a calm sense of patience in this experience. But before you get there, you must experience the situation and accept your feelings, then mindfully meditate on them to detach yourself from them.

Focus on the feelings of impatience you're experiencing—honor and own those feelings—then listen to what these feelings say to you to help you tune into your inner essence.

Perhaps your boss or co-workers are giving you a hard time or a business meeting didn't go as you'd hoped. Take a sip of your Zen coffee, with your own custom bean, and meditate on this for a moment. See both sides to achieve a Zen balance, a blend of harmony. Think about the qualities and characteristics of the bean for a mindful moment.

What would the Zen coffee bean do in this situation you've found yourself in? Be the bean of your choice; be the flavor of your inner essence. Brew your Zen coffee from the bean that brings you happiness and joy.

Actively meditating in a mindful manner lets you put the caffeine power of calm into your life. By looking within the qualities of the bean and the characteristics of the situation, you can mindfully meditate on the qualities of this particular experience and know what's important to you, knowing what you want to achieve through having this experience.

Be the feeling. Be the thought. Acknowledge it as a true and honest thought and/or feeling you have. Accept it, without judging, honor it by truly feeling it deeply within, noticing how the thought/feeling really feels inside you—what it inspires and brings forth, what emerges, and how it makes you feel.

Focus is simply listening, gently and attentively, to your inner essence—to your feelings. Be with the bean. Breathe in the aroma of your coffee; breathe in the flavor and essence of your inner self.

You can use Zen zippers—mini meditations—to zip you into mindfully meditating on what you are experiencing. Zen zippers are for everyone who takes their coffee, and situations in their life, maybe a bit too seriously. They're focused awareness meditations you can use in any situation you find yourself in—with or without your Zen coffee in hand.

You can zip into mindfulness by meditating on the qualities and essence of your inner nature—the qualities and essence of the coffee bean. Just as the espresso in your coffee gives you a shot of energy, the calm peacefulness of Zen gives you a shot of your essence.

Wherever you are, whatever you're doing, and however you're feeling in every situation you encounter during your day, simply breathe. Drink your Zen coffee and be present in the moment. Let your coffee zip you into the essence of yourself. Then wing it, making it up as you go along.

Breathe in the essence of the situation you are in. Smell the coffee beans; smell the vibes of the situation for a mindful moment. Be completely aware of how you're feeling in this situation.

Be present and focused with your feelings. Acknowledge your feelings. Accept them for what they are without judging them, without immediately grinding out a response.

In your calm, peaceful mind, brew the situation and your feelings about it for a mindful moment. Be aware of all the qualities and characteristics of the coffee bean/situation you are involved in.

Drink in the essence of your coffee; breathe in the essence and flavor of your inner nature. By drinking in the essence of your inner self, you will intuitively know how to brew your own mindful meditation that will work best for you in any situation to ensure a peaceful outcome.

Just as the qualities and characteristics of each coffee bean are infinite, so are the many ways you can mindfully meditate in any and all situations.

Bring out the essence of the bean, the inner essence of you, into your coffee cup of life. Flavor all your experiences with Zen coffee to make your life mindful in every moment.

Mindfully meditating brings you peace, calm, happiness, and harmony. It puts you in touch with and in tune with your inner essence as you drink in the Zen of coffee to flavor your life.

Zen coffee is simply being in the present moment, enjoying the moment—whatever is happening in the moment—to bring you into the peacefulness of a mindful moment.

Zen coffee brings forth the Zen nature within you; it brings forth the inner essence of yourself and flavors every experience you have in the coffee cup of life.

Jazzed Out of Zen

How often do we forget to be present?

How many times have we jazzed our
minds out of Zen... not being able
to see the coffee for the beans?

We do lots of things other than being present
and centering our attention on the present
moment because we have too many thoughts
running here and there, way too many things to
do, and we scatter our focus in all directions,
throwing our energy into the wind.

It happens to all of us.

We don't forget to be present. We're just not aware
that we're in the present moment. We forget to be
mindful of it. So, just be here, breathing and being
present, mindfully enjoying a cup of Zen coffee.

Chapter Twenty-One

Hot and Steamy

Is your coffee cup of life filled to the brim? Is it filled with anxieties, worries, and problems or is it filled with happiness, joy, and serenity?

Are you frothing at the mouth? Steaming mad about something that has happened or something someone has done to you? Trying to blow off steam to be calm under pressure? While these wouldn't appear to be Zen-like qualities at first glance, look deeper. Zen coffee fits in perfectly with all the stresses and problems you experience and encounter.

Just like the milk that is steamed and frothed for your coffee drink, you can blow off steam that builds up inside you in a mindful manner to bring you into a Zen peacefulness, into a pattern of loving kindness.

The process of steaming milk—through a steaming wand that is attached to the espresso machine—is accomplished by adding hot air to make the milk creamier and lighter. The steaming wand sends hot air out of four tiny holes in the tip of the wand. When these hot air holes are on the surface of the milk, they create tiny bubbles which cause the milk to become light and airy, and to increase in volume. By blowing off steam, you can experience a light and airy, carefree state of mind.

As the wand steams the milk, it activates the natural sugars in the milk. Steamed milk is sweeter than cold milk. Steaming brings sweetness; this is another Zen koan. You can experience a sweetness of mind while you are steaming with a negative emotion by focusing on what you want to achieve once you steam through the experience that caused you to become upset.

Suppose you're more than steaming mad about something someone said or did to you; perhaps you're frothing about it—agitating yourself into a stressful frame of mind. Let the light, airy froth of your Zen coffee drink lift you out of your despair. Milk expands when it is steamed; your negativity will expand the longer you focus on it.

Steamed milk is the thick, hot, liquid portion of the milk that helps to create the froth. The frothed milk that tops your coffee drink is not really a liquid; it's more like foam—a light, airy substance.

Foam is the top layer of the small, creamy bubbles that form on the surface of the steamed milk. This is accomplished by lowering the pitcher the milk is being steamed in so the wand is closer to the top and can create the bubbles on the surface.

Once the milk is steamed—once you're done steaming about whatever it is that has deeply bothered you—the wand is higher in the pitcher so that it can create the foam.

Your mind is calmer because you're higher into your peaceful essence and you're through steaming. The negative emotions you were feeling have become light, tiny little bubbles of air.

Creating perfect froth is a mindful art. It's accomplished by keeping the steaming wand just below the surface of the milk once it has been steamed. Steaming and foaming milk needs to be done at the right temperature and in the right order. Steam first to 130 degrees, then froth to 160 degrees.

Take a mindful minute to really feel the negative emotion you're experiencing, then allow yourself to lighten up.

By the time the milk is steamed and frothed, you've achieved a Zen state of mind, which you can then pour into your coffee drink in perfect proportions, scooping the lightness of the froth over your peaceful Zen coffee and creating what is called latte art; a pattern or design in the frothed milk that tops your coffee.

Another facet of steaming milk and creating froth is that skim milk steams and froths better. Regular milk is heavier and contains more fat. Because skim milk has less fat, it is easier to infuse more hot air into the milk.

Be mindfully skinny about things that bother you; it's easier to create the light, airy, frothy state of mind where you can let any negativity go.

When milk is being frothed, it makes a hissing or spitting noise. When you're done steaming, your mind can release the hissing, spitting noises of negativity into a calm, peaceful, airy Zen froth.

When you hear the hissing, spitting noises, the froth begins to thicken and starts to rise, as you let go of whatever is bothering you to create lightness of mind.

When the steamed milk and froth are ready to be poured into your Zen coffee, swirl the steamed milk to keep the froth and steamed milk mixed. This creates a thick, creamy, foamy consistency with lots of tiny, light bubbles.

Swirl the steamy experiences through your mind to blend them into mindful awareness, to combine them into a complete experience, infusing the lightness of Zen into a negative experience to blend it into a positive outcome.

Let the feelings you have swirl through you, being mindfully present with them, then remove the steaming agent and be detached from the experience—whatever it may be, whether it's fighting with friends, family, your boss, co-workers, or a situation that has caused you to be upset or angry. Breathe.

Breathe in the energy of your feelings. Let them swirl through you just as steamed milk swirls through espresso when it is poured into a coffee drink.

As your feelings swirl through you and rise to the surface, create a pattern on the top of your feelings that is pleasing to you; create an image in your mind that reflects the Zen qualities of your peaceful inner nature.

When you are done steaming, breathe out this peaceful Zen image, then offer your fighting companion a cup of coffee, complete with beautiful, light, foamy artwork that reflects your Zen nature.

When steaming milk, just as when you're steaming about an experience, you shouldn't steam it twice. It won't froth and it will be scalded or burned.

Once you're done steaming, simply let go of whatever is bothering you. Make it foam; let it be light and airy; blow it off. If you keep it with you, churning it over in your mind, it will scald, burn, and hurt your Zen peace of mind.

Zen encompasses and embraces negative emotions and thoughts. These are all part of coming into balance. Bringing anger and negativity up to the surface is a natural, healthy process.

You can experience negativity in a mindful manner, being completely aware of and accepting your feeling—whatever the negativity is and however it feels inside you—without judging it. Simply accept it and see what it is showing you.

While negative thoughts and emotions appear to be strong, maybe at times seeming to overwhelm you, your inner essence is much more powerful and strong in a gentle, peaceful manner.

Your inner nature is self-healing, self-renewing in every moment. You can accelerate calm peacefulness by being mindful of and in tune with your inner essence.

The nature of achieving balance and harmony is to flow in harmony with the duality of every situation. There is a time of activity and a time of letting go—effort followed by receptivity; blending the duality into one—into unity and harmony.

Experience the anger, the frustration, or whatever emotion you're feeling that has you steamed. Be with the feeling; acknowledge it and listen to it. Let it flow and swirl through you, seeing what it is telling you and showing you. Then detach from it and let it go.

When you're done steaming, you can make peace inside your mind with the experience and feel a pattern of harmony as you enjoy your Zen coffee. Every negative emotion you feel hurts you.

It's important to bring your inner and outer essence into harmony. This is done by breathing, accepting the negativity that is part of you, being calm, letting go, forgiving, blessing, and feeling love and kindness toward the person or situation you first responded to in a hot and steamy manner.

Take deep, cleansing, renewing, nourishing breaths. Breathe in the positive, breathe out the negative.

By first embracing the negativity, letting it swirl through you to bring you into balance and harmony, this seeming paradox brings you into a loving kindness frame of mind.

Chapter Twenty-Two

Loving Kindness

You are filled with the qualities of peace, love, joy, compassion, and kindness. When uncomfortable situations arise or when someone has made you angry, you need to remind yourself of these beautiful inner qualities you possess and can share with everyone around you and in every situation you are in. You can mindfully bring these inner qualities out into your world and spread a lot of loving kindness around.

When you find yourself getting angry at someone or feeling frustrated in a particular experience, be mindfully aware of how you're feeling and know that you have the ever-present choice to respond to that person or situation with loving kindness. Take a moment or two to breathe in and smell the coffee.

In Zen coffee philosophy, stirring just a smidge of loving kindness into the coffee cup of all your experiences produces a perfect blend of calm coffee flavored with peacefulness and kindness.

Breathe in the peaceful qualities that are within you and feel kindness toward the person who has made you angry or the situation that brought you stress. Breathe out that loving kindness that is within you.

A loving kindness meditation is done in five parts, culminating in a blending together of all the parts into a whole. In the first part, feel loving kindness towards yourself. Become aware of yourself and focus on feelings of peace, calm, and tranquility. Then let these feelings grow into love within your heart.

In the second part, think of a good friend. Bring the image of your friend to mind as vividly as you can and think of his/her good qualities. Feel your connection with your friend, and your liking and affection for him or her, allowing your feelings to grow and expand in your heart.

In the third part, think of someone you do not particularly like or someone you mildly dislike. This is a person you have somewhat neutral feelings about. You neither like nor dislike this person. He or she may be someone you do not know well, someone who is an acquaintance. Reflect on his/her humanity and include this person in your feelings of loving kindness that you feel toward your friend in the preceding part.

In the fourth part (and this is where loving kindness really kicks in and you may have to do some work on this), think of someone you really dislike, a person who has really aggravated you in some way or who is an actual enemy you've had confrontations and arguments with. Trying not to get caught up in any feelings of negativity or hatred, think of him or her in a positive manner and feel loving kindness toward him or her.

In the fifth part, first think of all four people you've included in your loving kindness meditation together—yourself, your friend, the neutral person, and the enemy—thinking of them in terms of loving kindness and spreading these feelings of love and kindness to them.

Then extend your feelings of loving kindness further—to everyone around you, to all your friends and family, your co-workers, everyone in your neighborhood, your town, your country, and so on throughout the world. Feel a sense of waves and ripples of loving kindness spreading from your heart to everyone's heart, to all beings everywhere.

Gradually finish the meditation by breathing and being aware that you are breathing. This is a very beautiful meditation because you open your heart to both give and receive loving kindness. You feel so loving towards everyone and everything that it naturally flows to you in return.

After you've done this meditation and felt it inside you, you've brought it into your inner essence and it becomes part of you; it becomes a pattern that tops your Zen coffee.

Stir loving kindness into every coffee. Let loving kindness swirl into and through every part of your life, in and through every experience, rising to the surface and creating a pattern of loving kindness.

You can do this loving kindness meditation anywhere, anytime, in any situation you're in. You don't need to find a quiet place, close your eyes, and mindfully breathe. Simply think the words **loving kindness**. The words will instill a feeling of peace, calm, and love within you, and will bring forth all those wonderful, loving feelings from inside you.

Let loving kindness be your mantra that resonates within and through you, expanding into the world around you.

Chapter Twenty-Three

The Zen Coffee Guru

A guru is a revered teacher or counselor in spiritual or intellectual matters. His or her role is to help you tune into your inner self and attain enlightenment and the awareness of your inner nature through the Zen practice of mindfulness.

A coffee barista is similar to a Zen master. A barista is a seasoned coffee connoisseur who takes great pride in learning about coffee and creating the best coffee drinks.

A Zen master is a person who pays careful attention to mindfully meditating. A Zen barista is someone who has mastered the art of Zen coffee.

The coffee guru has been hiding, all this time, in your Zen coffee. Mindfully meditating reveals your coffee guru. Your coffee guru is your inner essence, your guide into Zen coffee through the avenue of mindful meditation. You are your own best teacher. You are your own Zen coffee guru.

Zen coffee nourishes and nurtures your inner self. Your life experiences are your teacher, the coffee guru. As you drink your Zen coffee in moments of mindfulness, the guru within you emerges.

You can meditate with the Zen coffee guru, the wise teacher within who gently leads you into the mindful awareness of your inner essence. Be your own coffee guru, follow your true heart.

It will lead you into your inner essence, into that peaceful place within you where you experience nirvana—the attainment of a completely enjoyable moment that provides the embracing of an ultimate experience of harmony or joy.

Be mindful. Breathe. Drink Zen coffee.

The Way of Zen

Coffee has no words. No words are necessary.
Without words, you can tune into the
pure peacefulness of the Zen within you.

Zen coffee is simply being in the
present moment, enjoying the moment,
without any words to distract you from
the peacefulness of a mindful moment.

Zen coffee makes you happy and brings
a smile to your face because you are in
tune with the inner essence of yourself.

Let a smile be your mantra
for today, and every day, to bring
out the essence of your inner Zen.

Simply smile, and have a Zen Coffee.

About the Author

Gloria Chadwick lives in Maui with her dog, Magi. She enjoys meditating on the beach at sunrise, walking through the rain and looking for rainbows, and being a free spirit. She also enjoys drinking coffee.

She writes nonfiction books and visionary novels on reincarnation, spirituality, positive mind power, and meditation. She's also written several guides for writers and a few cookbooks.

Please visit **Chadwick Pages** for more information about her books—http://chadwickpages.blogspot.com.

Made in the USA
San Bernardino, CA
18 March 2017